Just
BEYOND
HARMONY

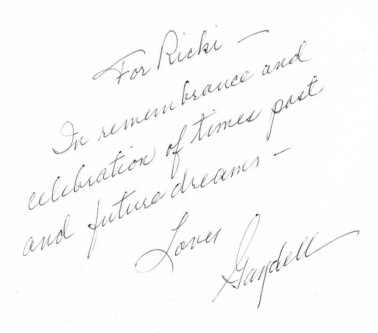

For Ricki —

In remembrance and
celebration of times past
and future dreams —

Love,
Gaydell

ALSO BY GAYDELL COLLIER

Co-authored with Eleanor F. Prince

Basic Horse Care
Basic Training for Horses
Basic Horsemanship: English and Western

Co-edited with Linda Hasselstrom and Nancy Curtis

Leaning into the Wind: Women Write from the Heart of the West
Woven on the Wind: Women Write About Friendship in Sagebrush
      Country
Crazy Woman Creek: Women Rewrite the American West

Just BEYOND HARMONY

Gaydell Collier

Gaydell Collier (signature)

HIGH PLAINS PRESS

Collier, Gaydell M.
  Just beyond Harmony / Gaydell Collier.
    p. cm.
  ISBN 978-0-931271-97-7 (cloth: alk. paper)
  ISBN 978-0-931271-98-4 (trade paper: alk. paper)
1. Collier, Gaydell M. 2. Collier, Gaydell M.--Family. 3. Frontier and pioneer life--Wyoming--Harmony. 4. Ranch life--Wyoming--Harmony. 5. Country life--Wyoming--Harmony. 6. Community life--Wyoming--Harmony. 7. Harmony (Wyo.)--Biography. 8. Harmony (Wyo.)--Social life and customs. I. Title.
                    F769.H37C65 2011
                    978.7'95--dc22
                                        2011011975

HIGH PLAINS PRESS
403 CASSA ROAD
GLENDO, WY 82213
www.highplainspress.com
orders & catalogs: 1-800-552-7819

FIRST PRINTING

10 9 8 7 6 5 4 3 2 1

Manufactured in the United States of America

In memory of
Conrad and M. Fidena Hansen
and in honor of
all the neighbors of the Harmony Community

CONTENTS

I began writing this book over thirty years before it was fin-ished while events were fresh in my mind. After drafting several chapters, I tried them out on a few readers and received encour-agement to continue. But life got in the way. Four active kids, work on the ranch, and a full-time job in town swallowed my time. Work on the manuscript slipped away from me.

Two events occurred to bring the story back to life. I found some boxes in storage that revealed diaries I'd written during the cabin years. And when going through my mother's things, I dis-covered that she'd kept all the letters I'd sent to her back then. Both sources recorded events I'd long forgotten and included details and dialog, much of which could be used verbatim.

Memory sparked and the years when we lived just beyond Harmony leaped into focus.

I resumed writing about them. . . .

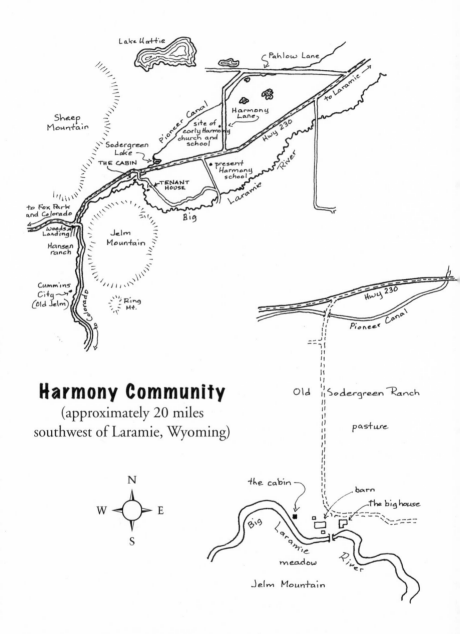

Lake Hattie

Pahlow Lane

to Laramie

Pioneer Canal

Harmony Lane

Hwy 230

Sheep Mountain

site of early Harmony church and school

Sodergreen Lake

THE CABIN

present Harmony school

TENANT HOUSE

Laramie River

to Fox Park and Colorado

Big

Woods Landing

Jelm Mountain

Hansen ranch

Cummins City (Old Jelm)

to Colorado

Ring Mt.

Hwy 230

Pioneer Canal

Old Sodergreen Ranch

pasture

Harmony Community

(approximately 20 miles southwest of Laramie, Wyoming)

N
W   E
S

the cabin

barn

the big house

Big Laramie River

meadow

Jelm Mountain

A LITTLE CHUNK
OF HERITAGE

W E KNEW THE OLD cabin was there, tucked back into the tall cottonwoods by the Big Laramie River. At the time, we were living in the tenant house on a neighboring Wyoming ranch where my husband worked as a hand.

Fresh green beans piled in the sink, and I was making supper when Roy burst into the kitchen, his cheeks and chin black with grease. He grinned broadly, beaming like sunshine beneath the battered Western straw hat. Sweat had stained a wide dark band on its crown above the bent brim. He pushed the hat back on his pale forehead but left it on. He'd been haying the native grass, grown lush in the summer heat.

Considering his appearance, I guessed, "You were stacking today, and at least two tractors broke down . . . ."

"A mower and one of the sweeps—but never mind that. Come see our new home."

"I'm obviously cutting green beans, I need to start the hot dogs, the rice is still in the box, and . . . ."

"Kids!" Roy yelled, his voice covering indoors and out-doors equally. "Mommy says let's go for a ride and see our new house!"

"He lies!" I yelled on general principles, forgetting the green beans. "*Now* you've done it. They'll think you're serious—"

"I am."

"—and then there'll be wailings and carryings-on."

Our four children, ages five to nine, appeared from vari-ous directions. "What house?" "Are we moving?" "How come, hunh?" "Where are we going?"

"Oh hush up and go climb into the pickup," I snapped.

Roy gave me a quick frown of disapproval. "Mommy means *please* go get in the pickup."

I tossed the paring knife into the beans, jabbed him in the ribs with my fist, and called the dog. Why leave the dog behind?

Peggy sat between Roy and me, her big German shepherd ears in riding position (cocked outward because they'd rub on the roof if she held them up straight). The kids sat in the truck bed. They had strict instructions to sit down in the box, not on the sides. The two older boys settled their younger sister and brother between them.

We bounced gently along the lane, crossed two irrigation ditches on narrow concrete bridges, and bumped over cattle guards. We proceeded slowly because Roy always proceeded slowly, which was fine now because we were less likely to lose the kids that way. The road curved west and the sun, low over the long, rambling bulk of Sheep Mountain, smacked us in the eyes. Roy pulled the hat brim low over his glasses. To the southwest, Jelm Mountain rose majestically beyond the Big Laramie River. Newly shorn hay meadows looked tidy and smelled fresh and clean. The kids jabbered in the back. The dog smiled ear-to-ear and drooled on the seat.

We passed a stately, many-roomed log house and a huge log barn with its complex of corrals and stopped at a tall corral gate. Peering through, I could see a cabin several hundred yards up ahead, framed by a thickness of large cottonwoods. Made of the same dark logs as house and barn, it looked overgrown and abandoned, but also snug and permanent, as though growing from the rocks and landforms of an earlier age. I sighed. The dog panted dog-slobbers into my lap, and the kids clamored out.

"Take your time," Roy yelled. "Careful! Slow down!" He was always telling us to slow down, as though he could arrest time and work it backward between his fingers. The big gate wasn't about to open easily, so the kids scrambled over the log fence, and I followed. Peggy trotted in elongated circles with her nose to the ground, pinpointing details for later study. The cabin looked square, and the roof sloped up on all four sides to the center chimney. An addition, which seemed to be an enclosed porch, ran the width of the front, and on its door, a rusty padlock held fast. We all had to wait for Roy.

"Too bad," I said. "Can't get in. Let's go home."

"Oh, Mother!" Sam said. The oldest at nine, he was tall and lanky like his father, and he'd already mastered the wry tones of a cynic.

"Just kidding, dear. Ho ho!"

I sighed again and looked around. Chipped concrete steps cracked away from the threshold as though shunned by the weathered logs. Wild roses ran rampant. Woodbine formed a mat of star-form leaves to the right of the bastard steps, and sprays of green tentacles climbed the wall and veiled the windows. I could hear the murmur of the Big Laramie just beyond the trees. It was closer here than at the tenant house where we lived. The burbling sound of gentle water lent a cheerful aura to the early evening, and my assessment of the cabin's setting moved up a notch.

"No key," Roy said. "We can saw off the padlock tomorrow." He tromped past the wild rose bushes that spread under the windows to the left of the door and went on around the house. The rest of us trooped after him in single file, the kids high-stepping through the weeds.

The cabin faced east; to its south grew a jungle-like greenery of gooseberries and more wild roses, willows, sapling cottonwoods, and burdocks, through which the suggestion of a path insinuated itself.

"Where does that go?" I asked, premonition pressing down on my shoulders.

"What?" Roy sometimes had selective hearing, like the dog.

"That path," I said, pointing. "Where does it go?"

"Oh, that one? Why, I guess that goes down to the privy," he said happily, turning to the double windows on the south wall of the cabin and jimmying on one of the frames.

"Privy! You mean there's no bathroom?"

My words disappeared into screech and splintery dust as the window yielded. The kids surged through like monkeys.

"No more trouble with those modern inconveniences," Roy said, ignoring the look I seared into him. We'd had trouble with plugged sewer lines in the tenant house several months earlier. He boosted me through the window and followed apace, leaving the dog bereft and whining on the outside.

We landed in the living room. The other large room in the front was the kitchen, and two smaller ones in the back completed the square. The walls, covered with papered wallboard, made the interior décor conventional rather than rustic. Pity. Double windows in the east wall looked into the enclosed porch. The only exit went from the kitchen door through the porch to the outside. A musky odor suggested tenants other than humans.

"Wow!" exclaimed Sam. "Will you look at that!"

Across from us, against the interior wall, stood a tall, elegant, heating stove, swirled in decorative acorns and oak leaves and intricate doodads. Its four bowed and rebowed legs had claw feet, and it was crowned with an elaborate copper acorn-like bulb, striated and winged in steel. I was impressed; Roy ecstatic.

Eight-year-old Frank's interest was more entomological.

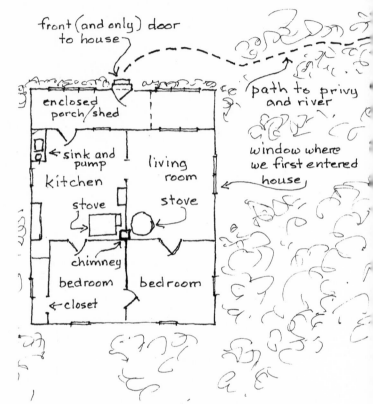

front (and only) door
to house
enclosed porch/shed
path to privy and river
← sink and pump
living room
window where we first entered house
kitchen
stove
stove
chimney
bedroom
bedroom
← closet

"Hey, Ma, look at this," he enthused. A black, beetle-like bug was crawling along the baseboard. Frank was of shorter, stockier build than Sam, more like both his grandfathers. He had a rollicking sense of humor and usually wore an impish grin.

"Ummm," I said.

"Scarabaeidae," he said. "A scarab beetle. This is a good specimen. I need a better *Coleoptera.*" He scooped it up.

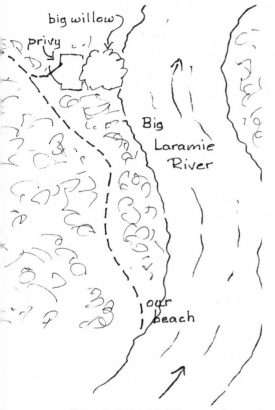

"Lovely," I said. "Do you have something to put it in?" His insect collection was growing daily.

"It'll keep in my pocket."

"Will it survive?"

"Oh, it'll be just fine. They all are."

The kids fanned out into the other rooms. Jenny, seven, kept inquiring which was hers. She sometimes felt beleaguered as the lone girl. It saddened me that her hair was mouse-brown and straight like mine, instead of blond and wavy like her dad's and Sam's.

Roy and I progressed in orderly fashion through the rooms, which were all connected by doorways since there was no hallway. The two bedrooms each had two windows, which put the north window in the lone closet. But despite its peculiarities, it was a tight little cabin with a bit more space than the house we were living in. And we did need more room. As kids grow chronologically, their space needs multiply geometrically. They need room for things like bugs.

Roy and I had made it to the northwest bedroom when we heard a palaver of some kind taking place in the living room, followed by some crashing and banging around, grunts, and finally a brief canine *yeek*.

"What's going on out there?" I yelled.

The dog trotted in, all smiles and clicking toenails. "Well, she wanted to come in," someone yelled back.

Roy, Peggy, and I progressed to the kitchen. It was like stepping into a block of moldy green cheese. An old enameled cookstove captured my eye and saved me from getting seasick. One window faced north, and a window and door looked east into the porch. In the northeast corner, diagonally opposite the cookstove, a six-inch-wide counter and grimy black sink held rusty parts of something, possibly a pitcher pump. The pervading evidence of a variety of rodents permeated the atmosphere, enhancing the overall nausea.

"Charming," I said.

"Isn't it beautiful? Just look at that workmanship!" Roy was admiring the stove, peering into the warming ovens, checking the hot water tank on the side. It had an oven and firebox and a couple of other doors that were probably there for some reason. He patted the enameled warming oven. I inspected the homemade cupboards in the northwest corner of the room with a sinking feeling that they would inevitably be mine. Nothing that buckets and buckets of boiling water couldn't fix.

"Frank," I called, "there's a fabulous collection of spiders and other insects in here."

"Oh, Ma," he yelled back, disgust dripping from his voice. "Spiders are arachnids, not insects."

Thus squelched, I gathered that I could dispose of the arachnids myself.

Sam wandered through for the third time and stopped, facing a gaping hole in the wallboard. "Looks like it was punched in there by a fist, doesn't it?" he theorized. "Man, that must have been some fight!"

Frank came in to see and got punched in the shoulder by way of emphasis. He howled and began flailing, but Roy cleared his throat in that particularly meaningful way he had. As the boys drifted away, Sam was saying, "I can't really believe this. I mean, this is 1966, right? What's with this 1890s stuff, anyway?"

I couldn't hear any more, which was probably just as well.

Jenny came in and tugged on my sleeve, trailed by Freddy, the youngest at almost six, a smaller version of Sam without the cynicism. Jenny said, "Mommy, there's something the matter with it."

"With what?"

"The house!"

"There's a lot the matter with it."

"But the bathroom's gone!"

She looked so stricken, I perceived the problem immediately. "They used to have privies, and there's one just up the path. I suppose it isn't usable now, but come on, we'll find a nice spot in the woods."

"Wait a minute," Freddy said, even at five trying to grasp the whole thing. "You mean there's no bathroom?"

"Right," I said.

"No bathtub and no water?"

"That's true."

His eyes widened and lit up like neon. "Wow!" he said. "Hey, you guys! No more baths! No more washing necks!" He ran off shouting similar absurdities, which I didn't bother correcting as other matters were too pressing.

Back in the kitchen a few minutes later, I decided we'd better wind up the funny business and get on with real life. Anyway, the light was beginning to fade. Roy was gazing fondly at the rusty pump parts.

"You really want to live here, don't you?" I said.

Looking almost bashful, he pulled out his Bull Durham and started rolling a smoke. The overflow of loose tobacco drifted down onto the gritty linoleum floor.

"Don't you?" he asked.

I let it pass. But at the same time, I felt the stirrings of excitement. This was closer to what I'd envisioned years ago along with all my other romantic notions of the West. Maybe Roy knew me better than I knew myself. But those long-ago notions didn't pack the complications and responsibilities of four kids. Nor did they take into account the realities of hard work and exhaustion.

"Are you really thinking what it would be like?" I waved a hand in eloquent inclusion of pump, stove, privy, and related intangibles.

"We're not very rich, right?" Roy said.

"Not very."

"And we're not likely to strike it rich very soon, right?"

"Very possibly we won't."

"So we can't give the kids caviar and silk football uniforms and a TV for every room."

"You wouldn't want to even if we could. You don't want 'em spoiled and bratty and neither do I." I temporarily ignored the fact that they *were* spoiled and bratty. In fact, we'd made it this far without any TV at all, and the kids seemed to be surviving very well. The food bill proved it. And except for an occasional moon shot or state funeral (Kennedy's had been only three years earlier), I'd never been convinced we were missing much.

Roy said, "So why not give them a little chunk of heritage—a year or two of living in the past?"

"We can't live in the past."

"Maybe not. But we don't have to take everything for granted, either. Kids just assume that a house is warm in winter and water flows at a flick of a finger. There's a lot of history behind that, a lot of work and thought and living. It'll be good for them to find out what living's really like. Maybe we can give special meaning to a couple years of their lives."

I felt my arguments slipping away beneath the tide of his logic, especially considering that I tended to agree with him, up to a point. But you don't just move into someone else's house willy-nilly.

"What about the owner?" He was a rancher headquartered farther down the river. The cabin was part of the original homestead complex that included the big house, barn, and corrals we'd driven past to get here. Because the current owner was interested only in using the surrounding pasture and haylands, he sometimes rented out the buildings.

"I asked him about living here. I guess you'd call him a reluctant landlord. He doesn't really want to bother with it. We can stay here, but any repairs are up to us. We don't bother him; he doesn't bother us." I heard the approval in Roy's voice. He smiled again. "Besides, the rent's only twenty dollars a month."

The day had been getting darker. There was a ceiling light in the middle of each room and I looked around now for the kitchen switch. It was located on the wall opposite the front door. Not convenient! I flipped it and a fifteen-watt bulb fluttered to life. Encouraging. "But the *work* involved in even washing the dishes, heating the water, rinsing . . . ."

"The kids'll have to help more. They ought to anyway. Hard work never hurt anybody." The end of his smoke glowed brighter and then he said, "You know, it might be a good idea to know how to live without conveniences anyway. Just for a year or so. You never know when we might have to: the next revolution, World War III, a seismic cataclysm, something."

I pondered this likelihood only for a moment. "But you're over a mile from your job."

"I'll enjoy the walk. Or sometimes you can take me."

We were all massed in the kitchen again. At that moment, Jenny drew in her breath and pointed. "Oh, look!"

We totem-poled our heads to peer through the bedroom door and out the west window. A big buck stood not thirty feet from the house. Several does and youngsters ranged single-file behind him. In the sudden stillness of held breaths, we could hear the murmur and slap of the river, the evening song of birds. Washed lavender by twilight, the deer watched us, ears alert, bodies motionless.

Then, unhurried, the buck turned and signaled the ladies, who moved daintily back down the river trail. He looked at us again, not frightened, but curious and wary, and then followed them, disappearing through the trees. The sky glowed pink and orange.

Nobody said anything for a minute. Then Freddy asked, "Well, when are we moving in?"

FORTY WATERMELONS?

WE CAME BACK TO THE cabin early next morning with some no-cook provisions, soda pop and water to drink, a variety of pails, rags, cleaning equipment, and visions of comfortable country living just beyond a day or two's settling in. Roy sawed off the padlock, and the kids and I assured him that we could at least get a good start on cleaning the place while he went back to work. He left, and the kids ran down the path toward the river. I followed.

At the ranch where we'd been living, the river ran beyond the bull pasture—not accessible for daily visiting. Here it seemed a part of home. We could hear its murmur from the cabin, and a short walk, brushing aside or ducking under branches, brought us to its banks. I wondered how much the river would define our days.

Lush, dew-wet greenery bordered the path and opened onto a grassy bank that sloped down to a cobbled, ripple-washed beach. Here the river's murmur grew to a pleasant rumble, pierced only by the twitter of birds and the occasional squawk of a magpie. The air smelled fresh and clean, rich with the scent of earth and plants and water. Warmth spread through me.

I settled back on the grass and watched the action. Peggy plunged into the water, and the kids ripped off shoes and socks to wade in after the dog. Slow and shallow now, the river posed little danger for the kids, beyond providing them the glorious freedom to splash and soak each other. They shrieked with laughter. I relaxed in the sun and let myself wonder how this had all come about.

How could a dreamy East-Coast teenager have ended up in a primitive backwoods cabin a few years later with a quirky husband, four kids, and a swarm of pets? Back then I imagined myself galloping a fiery steed across unfenced prairie beneath open skies. How had this morphed into the crusty reality of never-ending grunt work combined with the joy of unimaginable beauty?

I'd been raised uneventfully in a neatly patterned New York suburb, in a loving family of artists, music lovers, and businessmen within the niceties of a common-sense lifestyle. I loved getting up before anyone else to watch the sunrise and wonder about spiritual things. And to write—to compose poems and mini-essays that expressed my deeper feelings about life, as well as my longing for adventure. My wilder dreams were fueled by voracious reading: stories of danger and derring-do from *The Three Musketeers* to Jack London to shoot-'em-up westerns. Mary O'Hara and Will James completed the picture, narrowing my focus to Wyoming and horses. I loved the wind (rare on Long Island), its energy, freedom, and unpredictability, and this added to the attractiveness of my imagined Wyoming. I progressed through the local school system and on to college in Vermont.

When I convinced my parents to let me transfer to the University of Wyoming in 1955, I pictured myself marrying, not right away, of course, a cowboy, or better yet, a rancher. My plans, though not my visions, were short-circuited when I met Roy, a transplant from suburban Chicago, a man later described by a friend as a philosopher-dreamer. He fit right into my wilder imaginings. At first, I embraced his visionary tendencies. After all, his fantasies about the West were (I thought) similar to mine. He had come to Wyoming to "marry an Indian princess."

Roy was tall, lean, and handsome. His 1929 Ford Model A Tudor, twenty-six years old at the time, was a chariot of the gods. The little car responded to his touch like a willing horse. Winter storms drew us out from Laramie east to Vedauwoo or west into the Medicine Bows, defying wind-blown drifts and whiteouts. We camped in blizzards, sheltering a hard-built fire with our bodies, savoring burnt-edged hot dogs. Roy crammed his felt cowboy hat on his head, turned up his collar, and sometimes even pulled a scarf around his ears as a concession to below-zero temperatures. I was enraptured by his sense of adventure.

But more than that, he was soft-spoken, gentlemanly, and kind, though sometimes thoughtless. We both enjoyed Beethoven and big bands, the same movies, good conversation. We went to the same church. We both loved the land and the Western mystique. I found he had a stunning intellect, which I never ceased to admire, though I came to mourn his lack of practicality. Just as much, I admired his honesty and integrity. Best of all, I loved his sense of humor. It's how we met. We were in the same after-lunch political science class, which most of the students slept through, thereby missing the professor's dry but, I thought, hilarious wit. The only other chuckles came from the blond young man across the room, and we soon managed to sit next to each other. The professor enjoyed an appreciative audience, even if only of two. We both got good grades.

Humor was as vital to me as it was natural. I grew up in a family that loved to laugh. My father loved puns—the awful, groan-inducing kind. My mother and grandfather, Pappy, had a built-in sense of the ridiculous that made it hard to get a serious photo of either of them. My mom posed with her skirt above her knees to show a crazy bow-legged stance, while Pappy struck a silly posture and crossed his eyes. Nana, my grandmother, could burst into rolling laughter out of the blue if a sudden funny thought crossed her mind. My brother and I learned early to laugh at ourselves, to laugh at life's absurdities, to laugh with the family.

But even while swept up in Roy's windblown view of

life, I did question it before actually tying the knot.

For one thing, he held a conviction that America had been in her prime forty years earlier in the 1920s and sliding downhill ever since. His favorite president was Coolidge. He'd rather dig a ditch by hand than use a backhoe; he'd rather ride a horse than drive a car; and if he was forced to drive a vehicle, it had to be at least a quarter-century old. He couldn't fathom — honestly couldn't comprehend — why any woman would want a vacuum if she had a broom. I wondered if that philosophy might be hard to live with.

And another thing, he was always late. When we went to the movies, we'd arrive long after the film started and have to wait for the second showing to see the beginning. If we went to a party or meeting, it was well under way by the time we got there. This annoyed and upset me. I'd been taught that promptness bespoke responsibility and respect for others. Could I live with his devil-may-care attitude?

Oh yes, I thought, I can handle this! Think of his sometimes extraordinary generosity! Think of all those other good qualities! After all, life will change if there are children. Their demands would temper and supersede his extreme tendencies toward impulsiveness or delay. Babies need attention *now*, not when you get around to it. Three months after meeting, on December 27, 1955, we married.

I was to discover that he remained unfazed. It was the kids — and me — who would have to wait. If we were to take a trip, planning to leave at eight in the morning, it might be three in the afternoon, even in the afternoon of *the next day,* before we actually departed. Roy said he never minded waiting—why should it bother anyone else?

But just when my frustrations built to pondering divorce or murder, I'd find another of the absurd notes he left me constantly, ridiculous, sentimental, illustrated with cartoon animals or antique vehicles:

Dear Little Gaysey, Your rather foolish dog, and your completely lovely self, could perhaps attempt to arouse your laconic (acting) mate (I like the term "mate," don't you?) at 6:50 a.m—if the mosquitoes don't get the job done first, that is. Please be gentle!

Once again, I'd put off wondering if it would be better to conk him with a frozen leg of lamb or a block of firewood and then either eat or burn the weapon.

In our first euphoric months together, we dreamed of someday owning our own ranch, and we never lost sight of this goal, although it was to lead us a merry chase across years and miles, receding as fast as we pursued it. But accepting the fact we'd need to take some detours along the way, we plunged ahead with life. Sam was born the winter following our wedding, Frank a year later. I dropped out of school. Frank was five months old when Roy graduated. We decided at that point, albeit reluctantly, to leave our beloved Wyoming for a while and return East to be nearer our folks, so the kids could get to know their grandparents. We drove back in the

Model A, beginning a five-year parade of cross-country moves with a growing family: Laramie to New York, west to Illinois, east again to Vermont, back to Wyoming and the tenant house, and finally here, a mile upstream to this rustic cabin by the river.

We first moved to my uncle's dairy farm in the scenic Grandma Moses country of upstate New York, a three-hour drive from my parents on Long Island. While Roy learned about milking cows, raising calves, and using shovel and manure bucket to clean the barn gutter, I discovered that two little kids could be a full time job, especially since I was pregnant again.

Frank was a year old when Jenny was born the following January. Sam, then two years old, had already developed an older-brother sense of responsibility. When family clustered to take flash photos of his new little sister, he cried in alarm, "Don't shine light in baby's eyes!" As time went by, he continued to exhibit maturity beyond his years.

Soon a gray tabby kitten adopted us. She had been living by her wits, the only one of her litter to escape the lethal intentions of Lady, the farm dog, by making a huge leap to our windowsill. Sam named her Toots. She settled in and became the feistiest member of the family.

That summer we moved to Illinois to stay with Roy's father for a year. Then, with a small down payment, help from Roy's father, and a mortgage, we moved to our own farm in Vermont. Jenny was eighteen months old when Freddy was

31

born in an upstairs bedroom in the 250-year-old farmhouse. The rambling structure had plenty of room for guests. My parents and grandfather visited frequently from Long Island, as did other friends and relatives.

The farm was a great place for growing children—and cats. Toots, of course, had come with us. Her frisky nature had a promiscuous bent, and she was usually in some stage of growing or raising kittens. Four kids under the age of five needed plenty of space, along with all my time, energy, and attention. To this day, the Vermont years blur together into a Seurat-like painting that presents a beautiful scene from a distance, all of which disappears close up. Time and again in later years, Roy would say, "Do you remember when—?" and then name people and dates, or pinpoint some bright moment from a farm auction we went to with all the kids. No, I didn't remember, probably because I'd been distracted by changing diapers, or feeding with bottle or snacks, or trying to find one missing kid without losing track of the others.

Sam helped keep an eye on the smaller kids, and often saved me from the difficult "why?" questions that came from all quarters. When I was fixing supper one night, Frank asked me, "Mommy, what do skunks do?"

"Well," I said, turning over some hamburgers in the skillet, "they, uh, well, they . . . ."

Sam interrupted with authority, "They spray you, eat, and hibernate in the winter."

End of discussion. Everyone satisfied.

We never did actually get around to farming the place ourselves. To start would have taken money we didn't have and couldn't borrow. Already we'd depended too much on cash infusions from parents. But we had a large "sugar bush," or grove of maple trees. Roy helped Kneeland, a neighbor, fix up our old sugarhouse and then worked with him in early spring when freezing nights and warm days encouraged the sap to run. At home in the old kitchen I boiled down some syrup, gave the kids each an empty bowl, and sent them out to pack it with clean snow from a remaining drift. When I poured the thick syrup in drizzles over the snow, it produced a caramelized confection. Or boiling it down further, I filled fancy tins with maple sugar for Christmas presents.

In the summer we leased out our pastures for a bit of income, while Roy struggled to find a job in the economic downturn of the time. But we planted a big garden down the hill by the orchard, and when it ripened, the kids and I trooped down to pick our lunch, corn and tomatoes mainly, maybe a cucumber, peas, or beans to eat raw while the corn boiled. At night I canned and froze and pickled into the wee hours.

Roy found auctions to be irresistible. I dreaded what purchases might result from this indulgence: rusty antique tools and machinery, boxes of old bent nails, and so on. Part of this tendency was altruistic: he intended to save historic artifacts for posterity. I was glad we didn't have more money to part with.

One of his more optimistic impulses led him to acquire three Percheron workhorses—a veteran team and their elderly companion—along with a tangle of ancient harness. He envisioned getting into farming the old way, quaintly working the fields with these gentle giants and iron-wheeled equipment. This never happened. Instead, he worked for neighbors or found occasional jobs in town. One of my favorite cameos is a scene in the old barn, where one of the big boys looked over his stall door at three-year-old Frank, who stood below. Stretching up his arms toward the huge head above him, Frank called, "Lean down and let I hug you!" I was charmed to see the old horse oblige. Frank's love for animals never diminished.

Our house sat right across the little valley from Mt. Ascutney, and the ski trails were busy in winter. Once in a while, the hills glistening under a full moon, skiers would take to the slopes with torches and yodel their way through the moonlight. We let the kids stay up to watch and listen. Some nights the *aurora borealis* turned the sky into a blaze of shifting colors.

At bedtime the kids lined up on the couch, Roy or me in the middle, to read a book. New picture books, old tales like Roy's *Danny Meadow Mouse* or my mother's *Uncle Wiggily's Adventures,* and later *Heidi, Hans Brinker or the Silver Skates, The Secret Garden, Misty of Chincoteague,* and all the others. Toots usually joined us.

She'd always been a feisty little cat, and by the time we'd lived on the farm for a couple of years, she'd developed a repertoire of tricks. I was always washing diapers, and I'd drape them by the dozen over the rods of one of those folding, freestanding racks, placed over the hot air register for quick drying. Toots hid among the warming cloths in hammock-like comfort, waiting for someone to walk by. She'd shoot out a paw, all claws extended, and seemed to enjoy the resulting shrieks. She found other places to hide, especially if we were looking for her for some reason, such as in the linen closet behind the towels, or up into the interior hollows of the sofa bed in the living room. Best of all, she liked to snuggle amid the welter of stuffed animals on Jenny's bed, where she remained quite invisible in plain sight, just one of the crowd, and could even watch our search with those huge eyes that blended right in with all the other huge eyes in the pile.

Toots continued to produce kittens. We were always looking for homes for her offspring, but many stayed with us. Before long, there were grandkittens: notably Herbert, a placid and amiable cat with a thick coat of orange fur. He grew to be very large, possibly because he was a connoisseur of fine foods—well, all foods. He would eat anything. To test this, I once served him a bowl of lukewarm sauerkraut, which he polished off in his fastidious and unhurried manner, picking the food daintily out of the dish with his right paw.

Toots thought her grandson was painfully stodgy. A party-pooper, Herbert always sat out her reckless attempts to stir up trouble. Then she discovered he was a soft touch, so took advantage of his kindly nature. Her first brood of kittens had been brought up tenderly almost to the point of full adulthood, but she soon lost patience with her subsequent litters. Once they were fed, she knew they'd get along just fine without her. She'd leap out of the box, tumbling kittens every which way, leaving them crying and scrambling. Herbert couldn't bear to hear kittens cry. He'd pad over to the box and climb in gingerly, sit down with care, and let the squirming bodies snuggle up to him. Sometimes he'd lick them into contentment and then, because he couldn't lie down without disturbing them, he'd sit for long periods with Oriental stoicism, letting his whiskers droop and his eyes close.

Meanwhile, the recession deepened, and life seemed to be getting ever more difficult. How long could we even *keep* the farm? While we tried to put a good face on things, especially for the kids, we struggled to make ends meet. Roy picked up jobs where he could, one summer working for a highway construction company building the new interstate in New Hampshire. I made a tiny contribution by tutoring high schoolers. My folks paid a dairy to deliver milk to our door.

One spring day, I had no idea what we'd have to eat that night. I felt like Old Mother Hubbard ransacking her cupboard and the now-empty freezer, trying in vain to find something for the kids to gnaw on for their next meal. Feigning good cheer, I told them, "Let's go pick dandelion leaves! We'll boil them up for supper." As we picked I thought of what I'd read in the Bible early that morning, my time to fortify myself for the day with spiritual study, even if only for a few moments. Jesus gave thanks first, then fed the multitudes with a few loaves and fishes. Could I see God's provision if it was right before my eyes? I tried to be thankful for the lawn full of dandelions. Just before mealtime, I was boiling the greens when Sam, who was playing outside, spotted a slow figure trudging up the hill.

"Hey," he called to us. "Here comes Mrs. Van Dusen!"

From our back step, we could see she was carrying something. Jenny broke into a wide grin. "Maybe she brought us doughnuts!" We often stopped by her house on the road at the bottom of our hill, and she always produced fresh-baked doughnuts for the kids. Jenny could be a picky eater, but not where Mrs. Van Dusen's specialty was concerned. Now she and the other kids ran to meet our octogenarian neighbor, and I followed.

Along with a bulging paper sack, she bore a large casserole. I was amazed that she had decided to walk up our long hill with this load at her age.

"Have you ever had red flannel hash?" she asked, pulling back a corner of dish towel covering the dish to reveal a concoction the color of Pepto Bismal.

"No," I said, then added with all the enthusiasm I could muster, "but it sure *smells* heavenly! And do I smell doughnuts, too?" I relieved her of the warm casserole, and we all trooped on up to the kitchen. She came in to rest a few minutes before starting back down the hill to her home, and we all had pre-supper doughnuts while thanking her profusely.

Red flannel hash, a mixture of mashed beets and potatoes, might not be the most appealing food to look at, but it surely smelled divine. Set off with the dandelion greens, the hash made a glorious main dish, and Mrs. Van Dusen's doughnuts were treats of solid ambrosia. Never had any meal tasted so delicious!

※ ⁓ ※ ⁓ ※ ⁓ ※

Vermont, the Green Mountain State, is hilly, and the steep hill to our house presented both disadvantages (impossible to drive up in snowy weather), and advantages (to Roy's way of thinking, at least). We drove an old pickup at the time, and the starter quit working. Roy intended to fix it, of course, but since we could always park on a hill and then start the vehicle by rolling and popping the clutch, he never got around to making the repair. I became adept at this myself, and we managed without a starter for months.

One evening he returned after a day of job-hunting and burst into the kitchen. "Guess what!"

"You got a job," I suggested with hope and enthusiasm.

"Nope."

Kids converged in mass. "You brought us *presinents?*" Jenny shouted.

"You mean *presents,*" Sam corrected. "That's different from presidents." The kids were used to listening to Roy's political monologues, and various misinterpretations drifted into their conversation.

"Not exactly. Come see." We all followed him out.

The bed of the pickup was piled high with watermelons. "Forty!" Roy exclaimed joyously.

The kids obliged with oohs and aahs.

I was appalled. I could even see a few piled on the front seat. "What in heaven's name are we going to do with them?"

"I could have brought twice as many if I'd had room!"

"Are we supposed to sell them?" I inquired. What in the world *else* could we do with forty huge watermelons?

"We can't sell them. They're not salable. A truck brought them up from Florida, and a few were a fraction soft on the tippy end, so the A & P wouldn't accept them. They were going to throw them out. Imagine throwing out all those good watermelons!"

"Oh my yes," I said, with sinking heart. "Just imagine." We spent the next two days driving around the countryside, doling out watermelons to neighbors and strangers alike. And eating watermelon at home.

But still there were no solid jobs. Roy, his optimism shaken, was building a restlessness that portended something—I wasn't sure what. One night at supper he started carrying on. "Lyndon! Now even Vermont is going to pot!" He never used real swear words in front of me or the children—instead he used the names of current politicians. Always attuned to and critical of the ongoing political scene, he felt this expressed his disapproval or frustration better than normal cussing. In fact, he didn't like to hear anyone swearing in front of women or children. Besides, he thought regular cussing was boring and showed a lack of imagination

"More people than cows nowadays. Look out the window at night and what do you see? Stars? Fireflies? Not any more. Now you see electric lights all over everywhere. Houses springing up like mushrooms. Mountains crisscrossed with ski trails and furry with fake snow. Highways squirming with headlights. Nixon! Soon there won't be room enough for kids."

He missed Wyoming. Well, much as I liked Vermont, so did I. My dreams of open-sky Wyoming had been suppressed beneath the necessities of everyday coping. But they kept leaking out, like steam from a covered but boiling pot. I missed the pioneering individualism of the people, a spirit that in the East seemed tamed and softened by time, perhaps becoming a little too domesticated, a little too easily settled into the ruts of tradition. I missed the vastness, the wildness of the landscape, the huge skies where you could see brilliant sunshine, scudding clouds, or a lightning-streaked thunderstorm, just by turning around. I missed the wind.

More important, would Wyoming be better economically? Should we even have left to begin with? Of course, we couldn't regret the years of frequent visits from my parents, my grandfather, Roy's father. The kids loved getting to know their grandparents, and later they remembered the good times they'd shared. Even so, the pull Wyoming exerted on us continued to strengthen. Surely, if we could only hold on a little while longer, in a few years it would be time for us to return to the West.

For the most part, my thoughts proceeded on their usual ponderous lines. Moving would be more complicated now with four kids and two cats. Toots and Herbert would have to come with us. We'd wait until all the kids were out of diapers. We'd probably need a station wagon for the 2000-mile trip, and we'd need to hire a moving van. We'd have to sell the farm and the horses and find homes for the other cats. Roy would have to see about getting a job. All this would take time.

Roy's thoughts, on the other hand, leap-frogged over such mundane details. He was ready to go now. We'd drive our two vehicles of long standing: the 1929 Model A (with her special Vermont license plate, MULE) and a 1932 Chevy roadster Roy had bought as a teenager (CHEV—but we fondly called her Susie), though they were nearing their thirty-fifth birthdays. He suddenly swung into action and listed our farm with a real estate dealer. This proved effective, and over the next several weeks he made arrangements with various farmers to sell the horses and some of the odd equipment we'd acquired. With this income, plus the down payment we received on the farm, he hired Allied Van Lines to transport furniture, barrels of stuffed animals, and such acquisitions from country auctions as a cream separator (pieces missing), the still-tangled draft-horse harness, and an open buggy, none of which he felt he could part with. And we had enough cash left to make the trip. We'd leave in June.

Once again, tuning out niggling forebodings and making assumptions, I drifted with the flow. Roy glossed over any questions I had with his brand of seemingly unassailable logic. Or had I unwittingly adopted some of his dreamy, it's-bound-to-get-better-somewhere-else philosophy? Things had worked out in the past, and surely they would again, even if I couldn't see how at the moment.

HERE? WHERE'S HERE?

I BEGAN SORTING AND PACKING and put boxes of stuff in the car for Roy to take to the dump. Mostly he brought them back in again. I thought we could easily discard the contents of the "culch" drawer—broken toy parts, bits of string "too short to be saved," single shoelaces, and the like—but Roy was appalled. "We might *need* that some day!"

I held up a rusty, nondescript scrap of metal. "What could you ever use this for?"

"I don't know yet. We don't need it yet."

I dumped the whole works into a box, threw in other odds and ends until it was packed solid, and labeled it "Hopelessly Miscellaneous." The moving truck came. One of the movers carried Hopelessly Miscellaneous around to show off to the others, and they all giggled. The men groaned, complained, and dawdled over the heavy boxes of books and records until I put a Sousa march on the phonograph that wasn't packed yet. They speeded up and even began striding in step with the music. The movers left, but Herbert had dis-appeared.

On constant Herbert-alert, we stayed over one more night with crackers, Oreos, sleeping bags, and tap water in paper cups, hoping Herbert would show up. Next morning we made a final tour of garage, sheds, barn, sugar house. Still no Herbert. We shed tears. He was probably sitting out there somewhere, patiently waiting for us to carry him home.

We loaded two kids into Mule. Roy folded himself into the driver's seat and headed down the hill. I followed in Susie, the Chevy roadster, with the other two kids. We were all pretty tightly packed in, considering tent, two travel cases for cats, a litterbox for their comfort, sleeping bags, clothes for the trip, and whatnot. What didn't fit inside was tied outside on the running boards.

Partway down the hill, the Model A stopped and through its rear window we could see Jenny bouncing. Roy was get-ting out.

"Wow! Lookit!" Sam cried. There in the road Herbert sat serenely blocking the way. Roy gathered him up and passed him around for hugging and fussing over. Jenny and I cried, Frank laughed, Freddy giggled, and Sam philoso-phized: "I think he did that on purpose." At last we were off for sure.

This was not a speedy trip. Some days we barely made forty miles, because Susie had radiator trouble, or Mule had a flat, or it was already noon by the time we'd loaded everybody and everything for travel. With unmitigated optimism, Roy had envisioned camping by night under the stars and cooking hotdogs over a cheerful fire. We tried it the first night. Darkness settled over us before the tent was erected. Then all six air mattresses had to be blown up (the little hand pump didn't work, so Roy and I blew). We closed the cats into the Model A. A storm came up, blasting us with thunder, lightning, wind, rain. The air mattresses went flat, the kids griped, and the tent leaked. After that, we stopped at motels that welcomed pets.

Both cats had to ride in Mule, an enclosed vehicle, so they could be let out of their cases to move around. Herbert found his ideal spot on the back window-shelf. He'd lie there for hours, watching the world drift by, sleeping in the sun, or apparently disconcerting following drivers with an unblinking stare. They usually honked and waved when they passed.

Toots, on the other hand, lay grumpily on Jenny's lap. Sometimes she'd stick a paw out the partly open window and rake the air, probably hoping to attract the notice of passers-by, or perhaps the highway patrol. As a rule, Toots made enough trouble that the kids didn't have to. Aside from a brotherly bonk or scuffle, they read comics, slept in boredom, looked up when Roy exclaimed over a point of interest, counted state license plates, or kept score of who spied the first white horse, red cowboy hat, or Dairy Queen (a required stop). We hoped that Toots, who looked more pregnant every day, would hold together for the length of the journey.

She didn't. We went into a restaurant for breakfast and returned to find Toots purring contentedly on the back seat with four kittens. After some cleaning up and rearranging, we were off again. Really, the kittens were a great boon, keeping Toots occupied for much of the trip, until she decided that a moving vehicle was no place to raise a family. Then whenever we stopped, she picked up a kitten and tried to make a break for it.

Weather was kind for the most part, allowing us to fold down the top on the roadster and let one or two kids ride in the rumble seat, their favorite spot.

Our little caravan attracted stares, including the attention of the Nebraska Highway Patrol, which wasn't all Toots's fault. They just didn't believe us. It wasn't possible that Ma and Pa Kettle could make it all the way from Vermont in this kind of an outfit. That there were two outfits was even more unlikely.

They inspected our plates. MULE? CHEV? Come *on*, who did we think we were kidding? "Vanity" plates weren't common then, apparently not in Nebraska, anyway. Roy unfolded himself from the Model A, towered over them, pulled out his Bull Durham, pushed back his hat, and rolled a smoke. He answered their questions in a slow drawl, kind of the way Herbert would have done it. They inspected our registrations and decided they were "pretty good fakes." They checked out all the passengers. Toots raked her claws out the window. Jenny cried. Frank asked if we were being arrested. Herbert yawned. We had to wait while they radioed headquarters to put in a call to the Vermont Department of Transportation. Finally, reluctantly, after an hour or two, they had to let us go on our way. They still didn't look as though they believed us, *or* the Vermont officials.

Next morning, at long last, we slid over the border into Wyoming. Our little caravan rumbled through Cheyenne and chugged up the long, geologic "ramp" toward the Summit, highest point on the whole transcontinental highway. At the top, the Model A stopped, and I pulled over behind it. The view spilled away like floodwaters from a broken dam. It swept out across the valley to a far ring of blue hills and ragged gray mountains, the horizon capped with ranges of white peaks that dazzled in the morning sunlight. Overhead the sky of surrealistic blue rose into infinity. My heart swelled.

"Whasamatter this time?" Sam inquired, pulling himself up from a deep slouch. Excruciatingly bored at having ridden 2,000 miles at a high cruising speed of forty-five miles per hour, he remained unconvinced that an older car was better, and he was beginning to argue the point. Up ahead, Roy had disengaged himself from Mule and was in the process of extricating Frank and Jenny without losing Toots.

"We're here," I said. To me, this was home, and we had finally returned.

"Here? Where's here?" Sam craned his body to peer over the windshield (the roadster's top was down), making a show of shading his eyes. As the oldest kid, even if only going on seven, he felt it his duty to be cynical.

47

He did have a point. My elation dimmed as practicality nudged my elbow. I wasn't even sure where we were going, where we'd be living, *how* we'd be living. I remembered Roy's vague assurances back in Vermont, and that at the time I'd been inclined to go along with them.

"Look at the view," I said. "Did you ever see anything like it?"

"No," Sam said, unrapturously.

I reached an arm around to the outside door handle— there wasn't one on the inside (did I forget to mention that before?)—and stretched my legs over the wide running board and from there to Wyoming ground. Sam sighed and climbed over the door on his side. We all clustered around Roy. He smiled ear-to-ear as he tugged the Bull Durham sack from his pocket and rolled a smoke, turning to keep the wind from snatching away the loose tobacco. He ran his tongue along the edge of the paper, cupped his hands around the match he struck with his thumbnail, and looked out over the landscape,

"There she is," he said. "Home." He drew gulping breaths of pure mountain air between drags of pure Bull Durham smoke, as though resuming breathing after years of eastern pollution and population. To him, anything over two people per square mile was badly overcrowded. "That," he said expansively, "is the Laramie Valley."

"It's beautiful," Jenny said, not yet addicted to dripping sarcasm. Thanks to some domestically oriented Vermont neighbors, she was—for now—enamored of such feminine gentility as frilly aprons, fastidious fingernails, and bedroom walls papered in petite sprigs of violets and cornflowers. She had learned to cross-stitch and always colored neatly within the lines. The trip had been a trial to her when it came to creature comforts.

"And that's the Snowy Range," Roy pointed to shining peaks, as wind whipped at our clothes. "And over there's the Neversummer Range of the Colorado Rockies. That snake of gray-green is the Big Laramie River. You can see it shining in places, but mostly it's encased in willows and cottonwoods. And that's the town of Laramie down there." He smiled at me over the kids' heads, and I knew he was thinking of the days we'd courted, hiked, and camped here in Vedauwoo.

"Dear," I said, "Susie's boiling over again." Bubbles were gulping around her radiator cap, and she began hiccupping and hissing.

"She'll cool off on the way down," he said, patting the vintage vehicle gently on a headlight. I used to be jealous, but I'd gotten over it.

"Look across there." He pointed again. "See the long, gray mountain?" Heads nodded. Susie burbled. Toots yowled from the Model A. "That's Sheep Mountain. And to the left of it, cone-shaped and all by itself? That's Jelm. Our house might be right at the foot of it, where the river comes out of the hills."

I looked at him sharply. "Well, I hope it will be," he murmured. I strained my eyes and memory, trying to see through the blue distance. House? I didn't remember any houses over there at all, except for a few huge ranchhouses. And yes, they *were* huge—beautiful log mansions built by Swedish homesteaders, each one claiming its place along the river. Not the sort of thing we'd be moving into.

"How far over there?" Sam asked.

"Just fifty miles," Roy said cheerfully.

"Oh, terrific," Sam said. "Only a hop, skip, and jump. Why not unpack right here and carry our stuff for a relaxing little walk to unwind? Why not—"

Frank reached over to bonk him on the head. Sam grabbed his wrist, and they grappled, reeling into the roadster.

"Be careful of Susie!" Roy cried, as she started rocking. The incipient riot slowed.

"Oh, oh!" Jenny yelled, staring at the Model A. Toots, with a kitten in her mouth, was trying to squeeze out a window. I could see she was eyeing an attractive rock formation some distance from the road. Frank sprinted over to save the situation, and we were soon again under way.

In the morning, the kids, cats, and I stayed in the motel while Roy went off hunting for a job and/or a place to live. We hoped to eventually have a ranch of our own, but now all we needed was a place to settle down—preferably out in the country with freedom, privacy, and growing room—and a way to pay for it. He came back late in the afternoon with a big sack of Dairy Queen hamburgers and fries for supper, which kept everyone occupied for a while.

"Not to worry," he announced. "All our problems are solved."

He didn't say anything more at the time, or maybe he did and I missed it. A whole day in a motel room with four kids and six cats tends to blur the mind.

I always tried to put a cheerful—even humorous—spin on these adventures when talking on the phone to my parents, assuring them of our well-being and Roy's imminent success in finding just the right employment. I knew they worried. My folks hadn't been pleased with this move. After all, they had chosen the best community they could find to raise my brother and me, with good schools, congenial neighbors, and the benefits of an active arts culture. Once or twice a year, when my father could afford it, we traveled the Long Island Rail Road into New York City for concerts, Broadway plays, opera, or ballet. More often, we visited free or inexpensive museums, art galleries, the Bronx zoo.

A good community in which to raise kids was our goal too, but both Roy and I felt that suburbia wasn't the answer. Roy's extended family was mostly farmers from Iowa and Idaho. Only his parents had left their rural backgrounds to pursue business and the arts in the big city. His father was appalled that Roy didn't snap up the job he'd arranged for his son in the Chicago company where he'd become a manager. But Roy wasn't willing to become an eight-to-five "suit," wear a necktie, and sit at a desk all day when life on a ranch or farm could be so much better. His grandfather had prospered as a farmer. Why shouldn't he?

My rural roots were a generation or two further removed, but nevertheless I was also convinced that kids could best be raised in the country, close to the soil, working with their parents, knowing the plants and animals, learning to love the land.

With tolerance, my folks recognized the lure of the West that had grown in me since childhood, a wild seed that had somehow sprouted and flourished amid their carefully tended flowerbed. Though puzzled by Roy's seeming lack of concern for conventional employment, they continued their staunch, sometimes even financial, support while we floundered through our wanderings. They'd been delighted with our move to Vermont, deeply disappointed when we left. The assurances I gave them bolstered my own misgivings and wavering optimism, while I tried to ignore my uncertainty that our chosen path made any sense at all—even, in fact, that it *was* chosen, rather than a random bobbing on the sea of life.

WHEW! THE BOSS
DIDN'T LIKE THAT!

T HE NEXT MORNING WE AGAIN piled into the old vehicles, Mule and Susie, and drove southwest out of Laramie on Highway 230. Solitary windmills stood here and there, sometimes with a few tail-swishing horses next to them. Cattle and sheep spread over the landscape. A pronghorn appeared like magic by the side of the two-lane road, raced the vehicles for a moment, then sprinted away, white rump flashing. Roy had indeed found both a job and a home. He'd be working on a cattle ranch at the foot of Jelm Mountain, right about where he'd said we'd be when we looked out from the Summit. I was impressed.

I was even more impressed when we turned off the highway just before it wound into the hills. Our little caravan crossed the Pioneer Canal on a narrow, wooden-plank bridge, bumped over a cattle guard, and entered a sea of color. Lavender wild iris luxuriated in the dampness seeping from irrigation ditches. Half a mile ahead stood several imposing log buildings.

Behind them, winding within its escort of cottonwoods, the Big Laramie River bit into the rising hillside to form a cliff, and beyond that Jelm Mountain rose in monolithic magnificence. The setting for the huge log house was so grand it was chilling. I remembered passing it years before when Roy and I drove down this way on one of our adventures.

"Wow," Sam said. "Is that where we're going to live?"

"Looks like it," I said softly as we drew closer, trying to envision the joys of living in such a mansion. I was awed by its size. The house and the huge log barn on the other side of a large, open dooryard were both beautifully crafted with trimmed logs and dovetailed corners. Their charm almost brought tears to my eyes. Still following, I drove across another plank bridge and then I could see the road curving away to the east. Ahead of us, the Model A slowed for the curve, but kept going right past the house. "Guess not," I said, disappointment crawling through my insides. "Oh well."

We continued along the narrowing road as its turns and curves followed the general path of the river and crossed more irrigation ditches flanked by cottonwoods and willows. At the next ranch we drove in and stopped by a small but comfortable-looking home on our right. This was the tenant house we were to move into. A buck fence (poles nailed to X-frame "bucks") bordered the yard, with rangeland to the north, a bull pasture to the west, and the river beyond that. Birds milled and warbled in the river foliage, magpies flew about in their formal black-and-white attire, and the mosquitoes swarmed in like a warrior attack with full barrage of arrows.

Sam started swatting. "Oh, this is great," he said, digging through paraphernalia on the floor to find the bug spray. "We'll probably be carried away, or die of anemia—"

Eventually we were all liberally doused with repellent, and as long as we didn't inhale too deeply and choke on mosquitoes, we were ready to inspect the cozy, modern, tenant house and meet the landlord/boss. He didn't mind cats, and his family included Lois, just a year older than Jenny, and Dan, a couple of years older than Sam. We learned that our kids would attend the two-room Harmony school several miles back on the main highway and that the school bus would come right to the door. My spirits brightened.

Toots oversaw the installation of her kittens in a box near the pot-bellied wood stove in the kitchen. Not that the stove would be in operation this time of year, but it was a safe and out-of-the-way spot. Next day, our furniture arrived—it had been stored by the movers, waiting for us—and we settled right in. The kids got to know each other, and Jenny was overjoyed to have *a girl* to play with. Toots inspected the house in detail, while Herbert hung out on a kitchen chair or the sofa.

When Herbert first went outside, he made it eighteen inches across the back stoop before sitting down at its edge to bask in the sun. Toots's first discovery outdoors was that our landlord had a large German shepherd named Demus, a dog who resembled her old farm enemy, Lady. Again, Toots leaped to the windowsills with undiminished skill. Her second discovery was that she was no longer a frightened kitten. Now experienced in imposing her will and formidable in her manner of attaining it, she set about creating a new social order on the ranch. Besides, she had a litter of kittens to protect. By the time a week had passed, an invisible ring had been drawn around house and yard. She and Herbert could cross out of the ring, but no dog or strange cat could set so much as a claw within.

I wished she could have been more discreet, but she didn't care how much trouble she got us into. One day, several of the men were working on some machinery in the dooryard — the large open area surrounded by the barns and other ranch buildings, the hub of ranch activity. The boss looked up and saw Demus walking up the road, glancing back over his shoulder, but moving right along. Ten feet behind him came Toots, stiff-legged, with her tail straight up and bushy, herding the dog home where he belonged. It was an ignominious display at an unfortunate moment. Roy said afterward, "Whew! The boss sure didn't like that!"

In early fall, Sam started second grade (he'd had one year in Vermont), and so began our official assimilation into the Harmony community. We were soon drawn into functions such as school programs and plays, 4-H, church services, pancake suppers to support the volunteer fire department, and PTS meetings (Parent-Teacher Social, the community's equivalent of the PTA), all of which took place in the schoolhouse and included everybody, babies to great-grandparents. The whole community participated, whether or not the family had children, creating lively discussions, like the time it took four months to decide whether to buy mats for calisthenics, what kind, how much to spend, where to get them, and who should make the purchase. We began to get acquainted with our far-flung neighbors, most of whom were ranchers.

The school basement contained the kitchen and a large open area that served as lunchroom, gym when outdoor recess wasn't possible (not often), and meeting room for all the school and community activities. The kitchen was run by Emma, a hearty and amply built woman ("my family was always working folks") known for being the best cook in the countryside. She made everything from scratch, right on down to the hamburger buns. Not only did the scholars eat like kings, but often ranchers and neighbors ate there too, just so long as they let Emma know ahead of time and paid a nominal fee. Her skinny husband, Chuck, was school bus driver, janitor, groundskeeper, repairman, and jack-of-all-trades. In addition to his normal duties, he took care of abnormal ones, such as evicting the skunk that, no doubt enticed by the smells of Emma's cooking, wandered in one warm day when the door was open.

To occupy youngsters while meetings were in progress, Chuck sometimes set up a big screen in a classroom upstairs and started the movie projector. A local bachelor, affectionately and politically incorrectly known as Benny the Jap, always joined the kids for the movies, the lone adult in a sea of youngsters, laughing as heartily as the rest. He never said much and it was hard to understand what he did say. He'd spent his early years in the Heart Mountain relocation camp during the Japanese internments of World War II.

Benny raised cattle, which he herded with his pickup truck, driving his mechanical horse through ditches, over rocks, and back and forth across the highway, until it got stuck or broke down, at which point he'd leave it and walk. In winter, we sometimes saw a trail of footprints in the snow alongside the highway, all the way from Laramie until they cut through a fence and across the rangeland, and we knew Benny was walking the twenty miles home again.

I was told his bachelor quarters had shrunk to one room. The rest of his large old log ranchhouse had filled up with junk. He nested there with his cats, and it seemed that room, too, was filling up with stacked magazines. Benny weathered any circumstance—political, economic, drought, storm, breakdown—with apparent equanimity. One neighbor said that if disaster struck and times really got tough, we'd all survive if we just hung out with Benny.

Once, when I stopped by his place to give him a plate of cookies, he didn't seem to be home, though his battered pickup was parked in the yard. I opened its door to leave the cookies in the cab. The seat was littered with magazines and papers: *U.S. News and World Report,* the *Wall Street Journal, Time,*

Business Week. Benny was more complex than I'd realized.

Before Wyoming schools reorganized in 1969, each district had its own locally elected school board, which hired teachers, chose textbooks, and oversaw the process of education. The folks here were suspicious of bright new graduates who waltzed in with crisp certificates in hand. Though willing to give the neophytes a chance, the locals held off approval until competence had been demonstrated. There tended to be a high turnover of new teachers. Some presented themselves as enlightening saviors to the rustic peasant population. This did not go over well. One, trying to demonstrate her capabilities at a meet-the-new-teacher PTS meeting, bubbled that she loved getting along with people and had been voted Miss Congeniality by her graduating classmates. She seemed baffled that stony faces greeted this exciting news, and I felt a twinge of sympathy. I wondered how thorough her education had been for teaching in a four-grades-to-a-classroom school, how prepared she was for plunging into a rural culture apparently as foreign to her as a tribe in the middle of the Amazon jungle.

One of the classrooms combined first through fourth grades, the other fifth through eighth. Sam was fortunate to start out with a teacher who had been there for years and knew most of the parents, perhaps had even taught them in her class. Mrs. Mathewson taught because she loved kids; she understood rural communities and knew how to teach four grades at once. The parents deeply appreciated her warm, no-nonsense competence. We heard that the students who graduated from eighth grade here went on to be in the top of their high school class in town. Sam settled in quickly and began making new friends.

At home, chaos was normal and moved along at a steady pace—never enough money, always too much noise and junk. We retired Mule and Susie from daily use and drove a '53 Chevy pickup.

At one point we agreed to take care of a friend's dog while he went back east to get married. As Roy and Mitch had been long-time buddies, I'd known the dog from before and had always liked him, except that he had a reputation as a cat-killer. This gave me considerable concern. He was a handsome animal with long fur in attractive multishades of brown and tan. To add more confusion, the dog's name was Sam.

Mitch drove in and parked along the dirt road in front of the house. Roy went out to greet him, while Jenny, Toots, and I stood on the back step. Mitch released Sam-dog. The men talked, and the dog stretched and began checking out the tires.

"That's a pretty dog," Jenny said.

"Yes," I said. "His name is Sam."

"Sam? Like our Sam?"

"Yes. I think we'll have to call him Sam-dog." (Roy insisted that our Sam was named for the dog, but since my great-grandfather was also called Sam, I'd been okay with the name for our firstborn.) I should have been watching Toots instead of Sam-dog.

What happened next was almost too quick for the eye to see. A gray streak shot from the back step, and both animals erupted in a cyclone of swirling bodies, flying fur, shrieks, and yelps. By the time the smoke cleared and the dog realized what had hit him, Toots was back on the step. No pussy footing around for Toots.

I thought she'd made a big mistake. Surely now Sam-dog would be gunning for her, so to speak. But her psychology was far better than mine. The very fact that he'd once been beaten up by a cat planted doubts in his mind. He couldn't concentrate on the offensive while having to keep looking over his shoulder. Besides, the whole affair had been very embarrassing, and he had no intention of having it repeated.

Sam-dog moved into the house with us, and Toots alternated stalking around stiff-legged right under his nose with making snide mini-attacks calculated to keep him off balance. While crouching on a chair under the table, she'd shoot out her rake-like claws and whap him on the nose as he walked by. If he turned to snap back at her, he'd bang his nose on the chair while she jumped lightly to another seat, snickered, and began washing her face.

His acquaintance with Herbert was equally baffling. Herbert was so good-humored and kind-natured that he couldn't conceive of an ill-intentioned encounter. If a dog rushed up to him, he assumed the dog was anxious to make friends.

He'd arch his neck and present the top of his head to be nuzzled. If this occasionally became rough, he apparently attributed it to an excess of affection. Sam-dog resigned himself to living with cats.

He did get into a serious fight once with Demus, but it didn't last long. Toots launched herself into the middle with such ferocity that the two principals each ran for home, leaving Toots in command of the battlefield.

After six weeks or so, Sam-dog went home, and the house had an empty spot, even with all the growing kittens. Having a dog around had been so pleasant, it hardly seemed reasonable to live without one. Roy had grown up with an Irish setter and favored that breed. I thought they were somewhat flighty and preferred a German shepherd. We decided that, as a consolation prize, the dog would be named by whichever of us didn't get our breed of choice. I had the advantage. Our neighbor, Ellie, raised German shepherds along with Arabian horses, and had twelve puppies at the bubbly, roly-poly, three-month stage. I'd helped Ellie with them several days a week and had already picked out a favorite. The puppy was more serious than the others, with marvelous brown eyes, an expressive face, and huge ears. Exuberant and playful, she was a rollicking addition to our household. Roy gave her the good Irish name Peggy, which was probably better than an Irish setter with my favorite German name Brunhilde.

Toots appeared shocked that after we got rid of one dog we would deliberately bring in another. But of course Peggy was far different from Sam-dog. She was young and malleable, easily taught by human or feline, and it took her no time at all to learn not to argue with Toots. The cat, for her part, recognized babyhood, even in dogs, and exhibited, for her, an amazing tolerance.

Roy's ranch work was seasonal. He was busy during summer haying and spring calving, but often his full-time help wasn't needed during the slower times. Although we continued to live at the tenant house, he looked for fill-in jobs, sometimes helping out other ranchers with temporary projects. One winter he worked at the sawmill in Fox Park, a twenty-mile drive up into the mountains. None of this was a platinum-paved path to fortune, however. I began to look for ways I could contribute a bit to our income, while still keeping track of kids at home and activities at school.

I'd always loved to write. Could this be a way to make some money? While in Vermont I'd written a small essay about driving from Laramie to the East in our 1929 Model A Ford with two babies, a piece that was published in a national newspaper. My parents bought multiple copies to pass out to relatives, friends, and all the neighbors on the block. And they bought a correspondence course in writing for me, which greatly improved my skills. With this for encouragement, I looked for new opportunities.

When visiting John Gorman, a professor Roy and I had taken classes from, I found he was looking for help in putting out an expanded edition of his book, *The Western Horse: Its*

Types and Training. He asked me to edit the revision. We coauthored an article on wild horses for *National Wildlife,* and he also asked me to take on reviewing horse books for *Library Journal,* since he no longer had time to do this. I was thrilled, especially since I got to keep all the books I reviewed.

I sold a few historical articles to the *Laramie Boomerang* and discovered that my horsewoman/neighbor, Eleanor Prince, was working on a series of how-to articles for *Arabian Horse Magazine.* Ellie lived alone in the huge log house I'd set my eye on when we first drove in from the highway. She raised and trained Arabian horses, feeding them in the great log barn and working them in the corral complex attached to it. We soon became close friends. I helped both with writing her articles and working with the horses.

All of this was good experience, but didn't amount to a lot in the way of income. Then when the community learned I could type, I was asked to type papers for neighboring high-schoolers. As a rule, this didn't generate cash, but was more of a trade agreement. I typed the paper (this was in the day of multiple carbon copies) and was compensated with something (usually I didn't know what until it arrived) — fresh cream and eggs, vegetables straight from the garden, fresh-caught trout from the river, home-churned butter, elk hamburger from the freezer, a loaf of bread hot from the oven, once a small Teflon fry pan. All of this was as welcome as it was useful.

Meanwhile, in spare moments, Roy indulged his interest in politics. He joined the local Republican Party and became county committee chairman. We always listened to political news and speeches on the radio, Roy with avid interest, me with resignation, the kids with varying degrees of attention (usually ignoring them completely). Of course, the Kennedy assassination made a big impression on everyone. Considering his father's political aspirations, six-year-old Frank asked, "If Da becomes president and gets shot, will we have a new father?"

One night in July 1964, we tuned in to a speech by Ike Eisenhower, which began, "I'm here tonight first as an American and second as a Republican . . . ," followed by the obligatory clapping and cheers. At this point, Sam announced, "Well, *that* was a pretty good speech!" He was disappointed to learn it wasn't over yet.

I DON'T HAVE TO
GO OUTSIDE, DO I?

WHILE ROY FOLLOWED his interest in politics, I dabbled in local history, rummaging through the university and public libraries for early written records. Even better, since we all loved listening to the tales told by some of our "old-timer" neighbors, I encouraged them to write up the stories for their kids, grandkids, and posterity, then offered to type them up in exchange for being allowed to keep a copy. Two of the men created many-paged memoirs that were published locally or archived at the University of Wyoming. I felt good about this, proud of my small part in preserving history.

The Big Laramie flowed through Harmony's history the way it flowed through the valley. An early *Midwest Review* writer extolled the river as "the lineal center of that ribbon of fine garden land . . . capable of yielding food for a dense population and of furnishing a handsome surplus for shipping." An overblown description, certainly, but like the Nile, the river's annual flooding produced excellent hayland and so attracted settlers.

For us, not yet attuned to its life-giving beneficence, the flooding provided a mixed blessing. While in dry seasons, the kids and I occasionally walked through the meadow north of the bull pasture to gaze at the placid stream, such excursions weren't possible in flood season. In some years, the water even overran the road to the ranch. The kids thought this was great and peeled off shoes and socks to enjoy wading. But this also meant the water table rose, sometimes playing havoc with country plumbing at the tenant house. One year it blocked drainage altogether.

Roy spent an afternoon messing around in a big hole in the front yard, along with a plumber and our landlord, trying to unclog the drains. Nothing much was accomplished by suppertime and his mood had turned sour. We were just finishing the meal when he erupted in his political version of cussing. "Milhous! This is ridiculous!"

Roy's sense of the ridiculous sometimes differed from mine, but in this case I agreed. Trying to live without usable plumbing seemed absurd. I didn't catch on that he meant *any* plumbing was ridiculous.

"Plumbing is nothing but trouble," he ranted. The evening was getting dark. "Besides, it's filthy. Why should anybody fiddle with pipes and joints and elbows and gunk? Fifty years ago people had sense enough to build good clean privies."

"There's still a privy out there behind the bunkhouse," I said. Most of the ranches had a leftover outhouse or two, just in case.

"*I* know. *I* use it. But you girls won't go near it for some reason. Just because you have to take a little walk across the road and past the bunkhouse . . . ."

I grunted. Sam came in after a quickie trip out behind the gooseberries.

"Starting to rain," he said.

"There, you see?" Roy continued, waving his fork. "More trouble. The water table won't go back down for weeks. People didn't *used* to be ruined by rain. It *used* to be that when it rained—"

"People got wet," I said, telling Frank to put on his hat and stay to the north end of the gooseberries.

"You think I'm kidding, don't you?" Roy said. "Well, I'm tired of this nonsense."

"Me, too," I said, with fatal insensibility. I should have known these comments could lead somewhere I did not want to go. Basic good-heartedness along with rampant impracticality often led Roy down trails I couldn't even imagine, much less foresee. Daily living could take on surrealistic overtones.

"*I* don't have to go outside, do I?" Jenny wailed, her legs wound around each other like pretzels.

"Jenny, don't look like that. Go ahead and use the potty, only don't flush it." We *could* get one or two flushes a day, proceeding with great caution.

"People are too lazy today—want machines to do everything for them. You won't believe this, but in town the other day I saw with my own eyes this lady get into her car—it was in her driveway—and drive five houses down the street—*five houses*—and park and go into this other house. Richard Milhous Nixon! I suppose she drove home and then did exercises all evening to try to trim off the fat. Whatever happened to walking? People *used* to walk. And they ate decent food and didn't sit around either stuffing or starving themselves and then being foul-tempered because they were either guilty or hungry. What's for dessert?"

"The cake right in front of you."

"I ate that. Don't bang the door! Don't come any further! You're tracking everything up!"

Frank stopped. "I can't help it, can I? It's raining. *I* didn't plug up the toilet, did I? You don't want me to *go* in the house, do you?"

"Frank, don't be fresh," I said.

"I'm not! I'm only saying—"

"Well, don't." I plopped another piece of cake in front of Roy. "Where's Freddy?" He was perfecting his skill of disappearing.

"He *was* behind the big cottonwood," Frank said.

"Oh, for heaven's sake." I went to the door and bellowed. Thunder grumbled like the bulls in the pasture out back, and lightning splashed white over the trees and the main ranchhouse.

A moment later, Freddy emerged from the darkness. "Whasamatter with sitting in a tree?" he said. "I wasn't getting wet."

"You're soaked," I said. "And you could be struck by lightning, especially under a cottonwood."

"I wasn't under it. I was *in* it. In the tree house."

"Especially *in* a cottonwood. They're sugarier than some trees so they're more susceptible to lightning. Go back and wipe your feet again."

"Then how come we don't tap 'em like we did in Vermont?"

"Because."

"Because why?"

"Maybe the sap isn't sweet enough."

"But you just said—"

"Well, I don't know why. Why don't you try an experiment some time—some *other* time—and—"

The lights went out.

"Aha!" Roy said.

The kids started running around, shouting. Kids always run if they can't see where they're going. "I'll get the candles!" "Where're the matches?" "The flashlight was right here somewhere." "Watch who you're stepping on, dummy!" A terrible screech. Someone had stepped on a cat.

Crash! Sound of glass breaking, liquid splashing. The dog sighed. Roy lit a match.

"Hold it!" he roared.

Action slowed. I found the flashlight and dug through a drawer of shoe polish, pencil stubs, stray rubber bands, and jar lids, and unearthed a candle. Roy lit it.

"Shucks," Freddy said.

"Don't run any water," Roy said.

Frank said he was thirsty.

"Damn!" I said. "There's glass and Kool-Aid all over everything. Put the candle over here."

Roy winced. He's the only one I ever knew who winced so you could hear it. "I wish you wouldn't say that in front of the children. Kids, Mommy means 'oops.' I've told you a thousand times—" He apparently thought I should invent my own original inoffensive means of cussing.

"Oh, shucky-poohs," I said with sarcasm. "There's sticky ol' lime Kool-Aid and nasty l'il glass splinters all over everything."

"All right, make fun of me if you want to. But it's important—Watch out! Don't let the dog into the glass!"

"Peggy, go lie down." She lay down in the corner and sighed.

Frank started groaning.

"What's the matter with you?" I shouted, spreading paper towels over everything and trying to consolidate the mess.

"I need water. I'm *dying* of thirst—"

"Oh for heaven's sake."

Frank's flair for drama sometimes combined with his rollicking sense of humor. When he'd first learned to walk—

and then run—he'd challenge me to catch him and then take off as fast as he could. This never lasted long because he'd start laughing and quickly fall to the ground in paroxysms of hilarity. Now drama inspired and intensified his groans.

"Well, why can't I turn on the water?"

Roy explained in his patient, professorial voice, sounding pleased. "This is modern America, Franker. Lazy modern Americans let electricity do all their work for them. When the electricity goes off, there's no light. The electric pump doesn't work, so soon there's no water. In some places the air conditioning goes off so there isn't even any air to breathe. Electrically heated houses don't have any heat. So in winter the house freezes and all the pipes burst. In a few hours— poof—you've lost everything. Nobody needs a bomb to conquer this country . . . ." He was getting nicely warmed up to the subject and pulled out his sack of Bull Durham. Its little round tag always hung out of his right shirt pocket, within easy reach for a left-hander. He rolled a smoke, dripping tobacco into the cake crumbs. "All you need is a wrench. Drop it into the electrical works and short out New York City, keep it that way for two days, and there's the end of the country. Please pass the candle." He lit his smoke and the paper flared up a little at the end.

I took the candle back, dripping wax into the glass, Kool-Aid, and paper towel combo. I'd already switched into "automatic," acting from the top of my mind while the deeper parts retreated into an all-too-frequent "this too shall pass" mentality.

"Why the whole country?" Sam asked.

"Because communications are centered in New York City. Stop the pump that keeps the communications water flowing and bang—no TV, no radio, no nothing."

"I'm not sure I buy that," Sam said.

Frank said he was still thirsty.

"Here." I sighed and drew him a glass of water.

He was disappointed. "I thought Pa said the water wouldn't run."

"There is still *some* pressure. When it's gone, the water *won't* run."

"Oh."

I finished mopping up the mess except where the wax stuck to the floor. The whole area was kind of sticky, but there was no point in fighting it now. Roy finally got up and I held my breath, because I could tell he was leading up to something, and I was never quite sure what it would be. Once he had even announced he was going to run for County Commissioner.

He said, "We are not going to be trapped by modern-world laziness. *We* are going to learn to do things the *old* way. No more of this nonsense where you can't get water into the house and, worse yet, you can't get it out again. No more dependence on plumbers and gasmen and repairmen who charge outrageous fees because you can't live without them, and *still* they don't do things right." He took his hat from the nail on the wall and jammed it on his head. "*We* are going to live like intelligent, independent human beings!"

He stomped out into the pouring rain. Lightning flashed, backlighting his tall silhouette, which disappeared into darkness as thunder rocked the house. I felt like I was watching one of the ghost scenes in Laurence Olivier's black-and-white rendition of *Hamlet*. Peggy rolled her big brown German shepherd eyes toward the doorway and sighed again.

This wasn't the entire reason for our move from the tenant house to the cabin, but it provided the catalyst, in Roy's mind, at least. As floodwaters receded, the plumbing and life both returned to normal. While I remained busy with kids, writing projects, and occasional forays into historical research, he was apparently researching ways to "live intelligently." I wasn't aware of this until that summer evening when he gathered us to go "see our new house."

 ❦ ⸱ ❦ ⸱ ❦ ⸱ ❦

The euphoria of that evening lingered the next morning as the kids and I returned to the cabin to clean it up and prepare for daily living. But first we ran down the path to the river. While the kids and Peggy played in the water, I had settled back on the grass to contemplate how I'd gotten here, all the cross-country moves and decisions. After that reminiscence, I began to feel the weight of this move. Just how sensible was it? Of all the turns that had occurred in my life, this was the most radical. Perhaps if I'd realized just how hard it would be, how much I'd have to learn, I'd have had second thoughts. As it was, some of my early romantic notions of pioneer-type living still held sway, even though the last ten years with Roy and our growing family had knocked askew my rose-colored glasses. While we kept our visions of owning our own place, now raising the kids to be good people held paramount importance.

I decided Roy and I were basically in agreement about wanting to build their self-reliance and responsibility. Certainly the framework of necessity would be a good way to begin. Chores would have a verifiable purpose, not be just a make-work project to simulate an active contribution to family life. But I doubted that Roy could see the overall picture when it came to the commitment placed on us, the parents, to pull it off. Especially on me.

At the tenant house, the river flowed through our lives as background. I was fascinated by the history that streamed with it. In an article written by Dr. Grace Raymond Hebard, noted Wyoming professor, historian, librarian, and author, I read that Jacques de la Ramée, a French-Canadian trapper and fur trader, entered the valley in the early 1800s. The name changed to La Ramie and then Laramie. "As a result of Laramie's integrity, his ability to handle men and to be their wise leader, both white and red men built up a lucrative fur trade. . . . Fearlessly the old trapper in the year of 1820 declared . . . his intention of going alone to trap on the river which now bears his name." He never returned. Some say the old trapper died there at the hand of Indians; others say "he met his last enemy at the mouth of the Sabille [*sic*] in Platte

County . . . where the stream empties into the Laramie." According to author Mae Urbanek quoting Jim Bridger, "he was killed by Arapahoes on the river in 1818 or 1819." In any case, he gave his name to the river, plains, peak, fort, mountain range, county, and city, the entire area "known even to so far away a place as St. Louis as 'Laramie's Country'."

Here by the cabin, the river became more intimate, more like a member of the family along with parents, kids, and pets—perhaps a wise elder always at hand to comfort and advise. I suspected I'd need the revitalizing power of the river in days to come. But a decision had been made, and the time had come to grasp it with both hands and good humor. Now we had work to do.

"Okay, guys," I said. "We'll come back later. Let's get busy."

MAYBE SOMETHING'S THE MATTER WITH IT

STEPPING INTO THE CABIN now presented a more daunting picture than it had the previous evening. Last night, I'd considered the prospect of living here first as another vagary of Roy's, to be taken with a grain of salt, then as a challenging but cheerful country idyll to be acted out for a year or so by our family. Today the prospect of making the place livable loomed in overwhelming graphic reality. Where to begin?

I decided to start with the kitchen stove. Aesthetically it was the most pleasing part of the room (therefore the most pleasant to work on), and certainly I'd need to use it shortly for cooking. I'd never used a wood cookstove before and had little idea how it worked, beyond building a fire in it. Maybe I should have asked someone.

I laid some crumpled newspaper and a few sticks of wood in the firebox, then struck a match. Smoke curled out around the stove lids as the paper in the firebox caught on. I fiddled with levers and doodads that I hoped would do something to encourage the smoke to go up the chimney. They didn't. The stove puffed, blew a few smoke rings, then belched clouds from the seams.

I backed up, fanning. The door and such windows as I could unstick were already open.

"Maybe something's the matter with it," Jenny said.

"Possibly," I agreed.

Freddy emerged from the living room, fumbled his way through the thickening haze, and shouted a general alarm. "The stove's on fire! The stove's on fire!"

"Don't be silly," I said. "There's simply a little problem with the draft." The dog, tired from her earlier pursuit of happiness, had been lying by the stove. She got up and left.

Sam and Frank converged from somewhere. They could always smell trouble and unerringly take the most direct route to it. They'd probably come in through a window. Once you start something . . . . We all retreated and stood outside for a few minutes while smoke poured out the windows.

Sam said, "Maybe we should eliminate *all* the modern inconveniences. Like the chimney. Nothing's coming out of it anyway."

"I noticed that," I said.

"Maybe the chimney's plugged," Jenny suggested.

I nodded. "Could be."

"I'll climb on the roof and check it out," Sam announced, but I grabbed him before he got away.

"You will NOT climb on the roof! You couldn't see

down into the stovepipe anyway. We'll have to take it apart on the inside."

Jenny suggested that somebody might see the smoke and call the fire department.

I hoped not.

Frank the Scientist thought maybe the atmospheric conditions weren't right and there was a downdraft instead of an updraft in the chimney and the low pressure zone would have to move on and a high pressure zone come in before it would work. Or vice versa.

"I suppose it's possible," I said, "except that women were cooking midday meals for centuries on stoves like that, and I never heard of *them* having atmospheric pressure problems."

"Fireplaces," Sam said.

"What?"

"They haven't been using stoves like that for *centuries* because they used to have fireplaces."

"With arms to hang kettles on," Jenny said.

I was never very good at this kind of conversation, and in looking for a change of subject, I became aware that one kid was missing. "What happened to Freddy?"

Frank pointed to a cluster of woods behind the cabin. One of the trees in its center swayed and fluttered out of all proportion to its neighbors. "He's either a mountain man or an Indian scout," he said.

The tree didn't look too huge. Maybe he wouldn't fall out of it and kill himself.

By now the smoke had thinned a bit. I went back in. Hazy but breathable. I studied the stove, which hadn't had a chance to get warm. My only experience with woodstoves had been with the little potbelly in our tenant house kitchen, the one Jenny always called the "hot-bellied" stove. It made heat, and I could set a teakettle on top, but it had no other function and wasn't complicated. If I were actually going to cook on this one, not to mention heat water for washing dishes and bodies, I had a lot to learn.

Clearing the stovepipe seemed like a good place to begin. I pulled over the only chair—the back was broken off, but legs and seat were sturdy enough—and climbed onto the stove, intending to dismantle the pipe. Leftover smoke wisps slithered around my ankles. The kids had all drifted away again, and sounds of intensive construction reverberated from the big cottonwood next to the cabin. Existence, of course, was untenable without a tree house. I enjoyed the relative peace and solitude of the kitchen as I applied myself to the problem. The pipe was together in sections; therefore it would come apart in sections. Simple. The only question was where to start.

"Why'n't you just take to smokin' a pipe rather'n smokin' your whole self?"

If I'd heard him coming, of course, I wouldn't have been standing on the stove contemplating the stovepipe. He was leaning on the doorjamb, skinny as a willow in winter, holding the Old Briar pipe I'd so far never seen him without. The

dog went wild—embarrassment, I suppose. She hadn't noticed him coming either.

"Oh hi, Chuck," I said, "just testing the stove. Peggy, it's
okay. Peggy, quiet. PEGGY!" The atmosphere was kind of
smoky yet. We knew Chuck from our years in the tenant
house. He was the school janitor and bus driver.

"I was going by and saw the smoke and wondered what
you was doin' here."

I climbed down. The dog went out to investigate whatever
news could be read from Chuck's pickup tires. "We're moving
in," I said, trying to make it sound like a normal, intelligent
thing to do. "I think we'll be here when school starts."

"Last day of August," Chuck said. "I was going to ask
you about that. Pick everybody up here, eh?"

"They'll be waiting for you down at the gate," I said
cheerfully, "except for Freddy. He's not old enough yet." I
hoped they'd be ready and on time once or twice.

Chuck looked around with interest. "House ain't changed
none," he said finally. "Ain't been here since, let's see, musta
been twelve years or more. Good stove, though."

We gazed at the stove, and I was pleased to know it was
good.

"Electricity work?"

I nodded.

"Remember when they put it in," he said. "Didn't have
an extra box and switch with 'em, and nobody wanted to go
to town to get one. So they put it together without. Can't

turn it off without you turn off the big house."

"Oh," I said, enlightened.

"Have to watch it, though," he continued. "Pretty elementary wiring job. Can't take much juice or the wires'll burn."

"Burn?"

"Nothin' to worry about, long's you don't plug in too much at once."

I felt a sense of betrayal. I thought the electricity was on *my* side.

Chuck wandered over to the sink. "That pump ain't gonna do you much good that way." He stuck the Old Briar he was holding into his mouth. "Ought to be fixable, though," he murmured, pawing through the debris.

"That's nice," I said, wondering how in the world the pieces could ever fit together.

"Need more shaft, couple gaskets. I kin put it together for you after dinner, if you want."

"Really, Chuck? That would be marvelous! I didn't know anybody would know what all that stuff was supposed to be."

"Oh gawsh yeah," he said. "We used 'em all the time. Always had to fit new gaskets or something. You need more shaft though."

"There's some rusty pipe lying around outside," I said. Chuck went out, looked it over, decided it would work, and then left, promising to return.

I yelled for the kids. "Okay, you guys," I addressed the assembling multitude which of course included the dog.

"Now hear this." I explained about Chuck and the fact that who knows, maybe *more* people would turn up, and we had to quit dinking around exploring and building tree houses and get this cabin into company shape. We couldn't even wait for well-water, I told them. Sam and Frank agreed to haul water from the river without dumping more than an occasional bucket on each other's heads. Jenny and Freddy took to sweeping up a storm, and I returned my attention to the stove.

Standing again on its flat top, I brushed the dust of at least a dozen years off the stovepipe where it elbowed horizontally into the chimney, then grasped it experimentally with both hands. It seemed very firmly put together. I tugged and twisted gently, hoping for a clue as to which joint might come apart.

Frank came in carrying a bucket of water. "Are we supposed to use the privy or not?"

"Oh, I suppose so," I said. "First let me take a look at it." The stove required more thought anyway. I wiped the dirt and cobwebs on my Levi's and followed Frank out. The day had heated up, but a delightful coolness lingered in the mottled shadow of the cottonwoods. Even though the mosquito season was almost over, their whine kept the air in ferment. I wondered how anybody had existed before the advent of citronella. Of course, when I was a kid, and the family sat in the back yard on a summer evening, we didn't need it. Both my father and grandfather smoked cigars, and we basked mosquito-free in the stinky smoke.

We followed the narrow, grassy path, hugged close by saplings, gooseberries, and wild roses. We'd have to prune back the young branches to avoid getting slapped by wet leaves after a rain. And I suspected the grass would soon wear away to dust. The path curved by some lilacs and met up with a rusty, barbed wire fence, along which it ran for a few yards.

The privy stood ahead, slightly tipsy, but sturdy looking under the protection of a gigantic willow that grew luxuriantly between privy and river. Water slapped against the tree's farthest roots and made sighing, burbling noises tumbling over the rocks. A big branch of the willow reached across the path, barring the way and inviting attack by ax or saw. I ducked under and stood at the door. The path curved on past the privy and followed the bow of the river upstream. I looked that way. Though invisible from here, the little beach where the kids and dog had splashed earlier beckoned temptingly. Not now, I told myself. I lifted the latch, and the door swung open, accompanied by the scurry and rush of something small, furry, and unidentifiable in the gloom. Sticky cobweb shreds waved from the open door.

"Oh, ick," I said, very glad that Jenny hadn't joined us in this first encounter. Frank was about to charge in, his scientific instincts alive to a whole new world of possibilities.

"Broom!" I said, forestalling him. "And shovel." He went off muttering something about scalpel and tweezers. "Rags, too," I called after him. I looked upstream again to feast my eyes on the bucolic river path and considered (only for a moment) abandoning the privy project. Instead I took a deep breath, pulled myself together, and turned back to look inside.

Well, maybe it wouldn't be so bad. It was roomy enough. The wooden seat appeared smooth and polished with use beneath the overlying dust and jetsam of time. The two somewhat differently shaped and sized holes offered a choice of seating comfort. The "window" cut in the back boards afforded a view of the trunk of the willow. Leaves had blown in and piled in the corners, along with other nest-like debris. Apparently an assortment of woodland creatures called the place home, and a faint, leftover odor of skunk pervaded the atmosphere. "Too bad, gang," I addressed the interior. "Moving time."

Frank dropped off the tools and disappeared.

Actually, it didn't take long to make the place presentable. A chickadee lighted momentarily at the window to see what all the fuss was about. I said, "Hello, bird." It replied sassily and left. I stood back. Not bad. Not bad at all. Airy, certainly—which was nice in summer, but not to be contemplated when it came to later seasons in the year. I closed the door and stood back further. Utilitarian, incontestably. And dignified. Altogether quite nice.

I shouldered broom and shovel, turned around and smacked my head on the willow branch hard enough to bring tears. I dawdled my way back to the house, rubbing my brow.

Somewhat reassured by the privy success, although making a firm mental note to get Roy to do something with the branch, I climbed back up on top of the stove.

Maybe if I lifted a little, the pipe would detach from the stove, and. . . . It came away from stove and chimney simultaneously, not in sections, but all together in one piece. Since I was still lifting, it had the effect of my trying to hang on to a flailing elephant leg. I staggered. Soot rained and began to fly. One end of the pipe went down, the other banged into the ceiling. Soot poured into my hair and down my shirt collar, lodging in my bra. The monster slipped out of my hands and fell against the warming oven, stove top, and finally the floor, resounding like cannon fire on the western front. It settled. I could hear the dog barking. I peered out beneath soot-laden eyelashes at a young man with longish blond hair standing in the doorway. This was Grand Central Station of the wilderness.

"Damn," I said.

"Mommy means 'oops'," Jenny said primly from the doorway to the living room, repeating what she'd heard her father say many times.

"Magnificent," the man cried. "I'm not usually greeted with such gusto."

A smart aleck, yet. "State your business," I said threateningly.

"Bang, bang!" From the bedroom doorway, Freddy had the broom handle aimed at the man's heart.

The man sagged, staggered, caught himself, and gasped. "Mountain Bell Telephone shot down at the pass."

Freddy peered at me, grinned at the telephone man, and then dissolved into giggles, disappearing with Jenny into the nether regions.

I jumped down into the soot and slid a little as it crunched underfoot. "I haven't even called you yet."

He grinned happily, having recovered from his wounds. "Saw Chuck at the turnoff, and he said you'd want a phone in right off. Since I was out this way, figured I'd save a trip, little realizing I'd be so amply rewarded." He was really enjoying this, and since I probably looked like a poorly made-up fugitive from an old-time minstrel show, I could see he had a point. However, the day was getting old fast, and I'd left my sense of humor hanging on the willow branch.

"Well, as long as you're here, you might as well hook something up. Only we still need the phone at the other place, so you better not disconnect that. And make sure it's the same number." All the phones along this part of the river were on the same party line, anyway. He looked around for the phone jack that had apparently been installed some years back.

Sam came in carrying a bucket of water. "What happened? What's all the noise? Fall through to an underground coal mine? Did I hear blasting?"

"What noise?" I shouted. My cool, calm control was ebbing.

He looked at me with a curious expression. The phone man fiddled with the hookup on the wall. Sam looked around the room and said, "I thought you were cleaning this place up."

The phone man made some strangled-sounding noises and his shoulders were humping up and down. I decided to ignore him.

"See that?" I said to Sam, pointing at the stovepipe. Not that he could have missed it. "It goes outside."

"Mommy means . . . ," he singsonged.

"PLEASE!" I yelled. I selected several tools from an assortment of pokers behind the stove and followed the trail of soot that was wending its way out.

Sam dumped the monster on the ground, and we attacked it from either end with our tools. The stovepipe was packed full of a lava-like substance, some of which yielded to our thrusts and parries. But the sections seemed permanently welded together by crystallized black ooze. After emptying several bushels of crud into a pile and opening a respectable aperture through the pipe, I felt better. Having slain the dragon, we shouldered its carcass, grabbed our weapons, and returned to the kitchen.

The phone man was crouched flat against the wall, firing occasional salvos around the corner with his screwdriver. His other hand held a phone and he was chatting into it, so I assumed it was fixed. "Hi ho, time to go," he said jovially. He hung up and wagged his golden locks at me, grinning.

"You folks have fun now."

"Goodbye," I said, encouraging him out. I even remembered to say thank you.

Climbing on the stove for what I felt must be the fortieth time that morning, I noticed light showing in the chimney and deduced that there was at least some sort of opening going upward. I jiggled the beast around until it fit into its setting, connecting stove and chimney, and considered the deed done. Nothing left to do now but cleaning the crud out of the stove onto the floor and then cleaning the floor, which I did—it all took a while—and then cleaning me. Or at least getting a start on that part of the project.

I went outside and yelled. "Kids! Let's take our lunch and go splash in the river!"

They appeared instantaneously. It seemed that "let's splash in the river" struck a more responsive chord than "let's get to work" or "time for bed." I grabbed the sack of food, Sam took the drinks, and once again we headed along the path to the Big Laramie.

YOU MEAN THAT'S WATER?

WE CLAMBERED DOWN THE bank onto the river's rocky edge, tossing shoes and socks and rolling up pants. Peggy beat us in and waded out far enough to get her tummy-fur wet. With the high waters of spring long past, the river had become a placid stream, only a few inches deep at its edge. Grassy banks sloped down gently to wide, rocky beaches. Cottonwoods hung over the river's edge and cast rippling shadows across the water.

The river cobbles were hard to stand on, especially now that the water flowed lazily, allowing watermoss to fur the rocks. Upstream and down, we could see only a few hundred yards until the river curved out of sight, leaving us our own private place, our own spot within the woods, with not a single evidence of mankind, nothing but the wind in the trees and the slapping water, the earthy smell of exposed soil, and a few trails of parted grass on the far bank where I supposed deer and coons and coyotes made their way to drink.

For all its tranquility, there was an expectation to it, like an indrawn breath or a quick glance over the shoulder, for who could say what the river would bring us, suddenly rounding the bend into our lives?

The Big Laramie flowed north from its headwaters in the Colorado high country, entering Wyoming and curling its way around Jelm Mountain to wind its way east past us and then out across the plains. From earliest settlement, water rights had been an issue involving adjudication by district and state courts within Wyoming. Around 1921, the United States Supreme Court, adjudicating between Colorado and Wyoming, determined that Wyoming was entitled to about 90% of the "dependable flow of 170,000 acre feet," Colorado the remainder.

Canals and ditches for irrigation had been built throughout the valley, their flow closely monitored by the use of headgates. The canal system affected the depth of the river. The Pioneer Canal branched north from the river a few miles upstream from our beach. In the late 1870s promoters organized a company to begin building the canal from the river northeast to Sodergreen Lake, eventually passing Laramie on its way toward the Little Laramie River. In another few years, the Lake Hattie Reservoir and Irrigation Company was organized, a supply canal constructed from Lake Hattie to Sodergreen Lake, more ditches built, and by the 1920s settlers were farming much of the bench country between the two rivers.

Midwest Review reported "no crop has reached such important proportions in Albany county as that of head lettuce. That region is likely to develop the premier head lettuce growing center of the Rocky Mountains." Although truck farming soon proved impractical due to climate, elevation, and drought, grandiose descriptions of fertility and bounty drew many settlers to the valley.

I'd already heard stories about "water wars" among settlers, involving bullying, fights, beatings, political maneuverings, even murder. In fact, I heard about fights still breaking out occasionally. But such hostile activity seemed hard to imagine as we enjoyed our secluded river-beach. While the canal water drawn from the Big Laramie accounted for the lower depth of the river during some seasons, this wasn't obvious to us. The river flowed past dependably and usually benignly (except for spring flooding), with a wide swath of shallow water making a natural playground at our beach. The swifter current occupied only the central part of the stream.

Now shouts reverberated. The kids splashed each other, and the dog shook while standing in the water, spattering all of them at once. Frank threw sticks for Peggy to chase and dive after, and she picked them out of the water, her jaws dripping like mini-waterfalls. I did what I could to wash the soot off, leaving as little as possible for later ablutions.

Finally the kids climbed out to eat, joining me for a few moments as I rested on the bank. We munched potato chips, chomped down Vienna franks from a key-open can, glugged sodas, grabbed an apple or doughnut. Jenny could be finicky about food, but the boys, Frank especially, had always enjoyed eating. I remembered, with a touch of nostalgia, Frank's first word hadn't been "mama" or "da-da," but "Oreo." Once we'd barely stepped into a country store in Vermont (he was three, then) when he yelled with flamboyant abandon, "We need Chinee noodles!" Now the kids piled back into the water. They tossed apple cores into the middle of the current to watch them begin bobbing their way to the Mississippi.

After a bit, I detached myself from the melee and walked upstream on the rocks edging the water. I felt very aware of what the river meant. Here was water, real water, not gushing from taps or hoses, not spraying from man-made fountains, but flowing from nature itself. Here was water to drink (boiled first, if need be), water to cook with, water to wash by. I felt primitive and safe and basic, like coming home after a long stay in Disneyland.

I moved into the current, balancing on the slippery rocks, faced upstream and flung out my arms. "Hail, Ganges!" I cried.

The kids and I finally dragged ourselves from the river and headed back up the path.

Chuck was already working at the sink when we got back to the cabin. The pump was now recognizable, apparently engineered from the bits and pieces lying around along with home-manufactured gaskets. He was just ramming a section of pipe up through the paperboard ceiling as I entered.

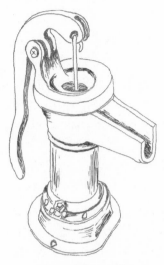

"Ain't long enough yet," he explained helpfully as the end of the pipe disappeared with a tearing noise into the attic. "Long as you're here, hold this." He wagged his left elbow, and I saw that his left hand was holding the tip of a shaft that went downward. "Take it keerful," he said. "If you drop it, it's gone for good."

Matching the pipes precisely, he turned the upper one into the fitting while I clung to the lower one for dear life. Apparently all was well, and he soon lowered the joined pipe, with his head cocked as though listening to its descent. Finally he nodded, told me to hold the shaft again, and attached the pump he had reconstructed.

"Now," he said, brushing his hands on his pants and leaving a tasteful pattern of rust stains, "now all we need's the water. Gotta spend water to make water." He pulled his Old Briar from a pocket and clamped it firmly in his teeth, preparatory to spending water.

Actually, the arrangement didn't look so bad, now that it was all together, except perhaps for the new hole in the ceiling. The pump was a little pitcher model, a cheerful red,

97

or it had been once and would be again, as soon as I cleaned it up and retouched its rusty spots. It sat on its own mini-counter to the left of the sink. Apparently the pioneers started with the well, then lined up the kitchen sink, and then built the house over the works. I was eager to see the clear, country water splashing into the antique basin, and couldn't wait to set a kerosene lamp on the corner shelf. How rustic and quaint!

Chuck had been pouring cups of water from a pail into the top of the pump. "Soaking the gaskets," he said. Repeating the operation at some length, he now said he was "priming it." He worked the handle furiously and it coughed and did nothing. He tried again and got a long-drawn sigh. More pumping, more adding water, more pumping. Finally, with a groan, wheeze, and gulp, it caught. A rumble, a gurgle, an eruption! Out into the sink oozed a black, sulfurous liquid of indescribable consistency and aroma. I retreated.

"Looks like the well needs a bit of clearing," Chuck said.

"What in heaven's name is it? Oil?"

"Just been settin' around coupla years. Stagnant."

"You mean that's water?"

"Oh, yeah. Bit thick."

"It does *not* resemble water," I said, on the verge of panic.

He examined the effluvium closely. "Looks like a critter or two might have fallen in and rotted down there. Prob'ly a skunk." The pump wheezed again, and another long-drawn sigh came from within.

"Dry," Chuck said. "Had about a gallon, though. Let it set awhile and try again. Ought to improve the more you use it."

"What! And pump more—uh—water in?" I'd already put gallons and gallons of Clorox on my mental shopping list.

"Uh-hunh. Clear up, too. Just needs workin'."

Meanwhile, the gunk had been slithering down the drain with reluctance. Chuck opened the cabinet door beneath the sink, and we discovered that the drain stopped as soon as it began, and the whole mess was collecting on the floor. Furthermore, a large hole perforated the wall, undoubtedly a main thoroughfare for the troop of furry residents with whom we were about to cohabit.

"Drainage system looks pretty simple," Chuck said. "Fix it in a jiffy." He gathered odds and ends of rusty pipe and fixtures that were lying around, both inside and out. Soon my sink drained elegantly out onto the ground, four feet north of the cabin—certainly a big improvement. "The boys can find s'more pipe," Chuck was saying, "and just add it on. Run the drain way out."

"Good idea," I agreed.

Soon after, Chuck exited amid my profuse thanks.

After all this progress, perhaps the stove would also behave now. Worth a try. I wadded up more paper and threw on top of it the little collection of twigs I'd gathered on the way back from the river. Before long, a fire was crackling mildly and the pleasant aroma of cottonwood joined the kitchen's host of contrasting odors. The pump burped, and I took that as a promise, rather than a threat.

I stood looking around for a minute. The whole place had a new aura of incipient cleanliness. Wouldn't Roy be surprised! Well, maybe not. He'd probably be more gratified than surprised. After all, this was exactly what he wanted and expected—the joys of simple living, in contrast with the complexities of the plumbing situation in the tenant house.

By the time Roy came to retrieve us late that afternoon, the cabin looked almost decent enough to live in. Sam and Frank had put dibs on a walled-off portion of the concrete-floored porch that made a room of sorts and would accommodate bunk beds. They'd cleaned out most of the junk by moving it into the main section of the porch, but we could deal with that later.

Jenny and Freddy pulled Roy to inspect the bedroom they'd claimed. Sam and Frank forced him to admire the embryo tree house, and I dragged him out to the cleaned-up privy, calling his attention to the low-hanging branch. Finally I pointed out the pump. I even gave a demonstration. I poured cups of water in its top and pumped with gusto. It ignored me for a long time. Finally it caught. I could feel it pulling up from the well, and soon it glurped into a rerun of the last scene.

Roy blanched.

"Chuck said it will clear up pretty soon," I said.

"Very soon, I hope. What are we doing for water in the meantime?"

"Boiling river water on the stove. See, the fire burns in it now."

"Isn't it supposed to?"

I'd forgotten that he'd missed the earlier smoke circus. Actually, I was almost feeling competent about the whole venture. Now that I had a chance to think about it, we'd accomplished a lot. Even the phone was in. The electricity might need a bit of attention, but overall, things looked pretty good. We left for the evening, and I realized I was looking forward to the next day. Roy would be off work. He'd borrowed a farm truck and rounded up some help to haul the bigger furniture.

Moving stretched out over a couple of weeks. Once the beds and furniture were settled in, we lived in the cabin, but kept going back to the tenant house for our books and all the paraphernalia of daily living. The kids packed their own things and then arranged them to their liking in the spaces they had appropriated. Quite a contrast to our move from Vermont four years earlier when the kids were too young to help!

I was glad, especially for the kids' sake, that we'd been able to settle into the Harmony community while living for those years in the tenant house. The transition to a cabin just a mile or so upriver was only a slight change in venue rather than a total blast of newness. It didn't affect school activities, our friendships, or Roy's various jobs. Although he was a mile or so farther from the ranch he usually worked on, he was that much closer to the highway and his drive to forest or town, depending on whatever alternative job he had at the moment. And at the cabin, it was much easier for Ellie and me to get together to work on our writing projects.

Roy and I liked and admired our neighbors and were generally pleased with the community and school. Our impression was that "Harmony" seemed to be a good name for both, if the petty squabbles and normal disagreements were discounted. I wondered if such felicitous relationships had been the reason behind the name and began looking for the answer.

Harmony appears on some Wyoming maps, usually in tiny, light print beside a very small empty circle or dot. And it turns up in different places. Sometimes it's centered on the junction of Highway 230 and Harmony Lane, sometimes on a spot a mile north of that junction, sometimes near the school located on a ranch road about a mile west of the junction. Each of these locations has some justification for claiming the name, although no actual town ever existed. A gas station once located at the junction was called Harmony Station. Harmony school had for many years been the focal center of the community.

But I found the location on Harmony Lane held the original source of the name. Around the turn of the twentieth century, a little church was constructed on that spot. One source reported the church was built "in an effort to establish harmonious relations between several church denominations." Perhaps that is accurate. However, since the community was made up mainly of Swedes and some Germans who were almost all Lutherans, that explanation may be a stretch.

The one that rang true was written by Geil Johnson, wife of Wesley Johnson, whose family were settlers on the Big Laramie. Geil had been an early schoolmarm at the school before meeting and marrying Wes. She wrote: "In 1907 the church was built adjacent to the school building. The leader of this project was the Lutheran minister from Laramie. Scandinavians in the community hauled logs from the mountains and did the log work. A cornerstone bearing the words 'Lutheran Church' was ready to lay. But one man wanted the name Harmony for the church and the people who had done so much work on it. The people agreed. The words on the cornerstone were changed to 'Harmony.' The man who had made the suggestion donated $50, which covered expenses of the change. The school and the community became known as Harmony."

In his memoirs, Wes wrote, "In 1905, the people of the community started a project to build a church. All of the folks interested were asked to help. There being more Lutherans active in the project, they took the lead. . . . Many helped to build the church, but the actual log work was done by trained log builders. The cornerstone was laid in 1907. . . . After a few years, the inside was wainscoted and the outside was sided with drop siding. These improvements helped to make the church warmer. It was open to all denominations and was a great asset to the community. Everybody used the church: preachers, farm organizations, politicians, and many others. A barn was built west of the church as many folks came to the meetings by horse and buggy. When more cars came into use, it was common for someone during a meeting to always be going out to warm up the car to keep the engine from freezing. There was no antifreeze in those days."

In the early years, the tiny schools moved around a lot, depending on where the kids lived. Classes might be held in a small log building, a room in a rancher's home, or an out-building on a ranch. Teachers boarded with a family, and kids usually walked to school or sometimes rode horseback. Often the buildings themselves were moved to a different lo-cation as needed, perhaps added onto another school building or serving as a teacherage. The Harmony church had been moved to West Laramie and became Grace Chapel before we moved into the area. The school also had been dismantled or moved. The brick building at the present location of Har-mony School had been built in the early 1950s.

Now the school bus gathered kids from miles around. On our route, the bus usually made a loop trip, heading out along the highway, then following the many curves along the gravel road that followed the river, picking up children from ranches on the way and completing the loop back to the school.

❀ ⌁ ❀ ⌁ ❀ ⌁ ❀

Our first days in the cabin, the weather smiled, heaping star-studded nights onto days of such brilliant blue that you couldn't bear to look into the sky. Late-summer growth luxuriated, wreathing the cabin in woodbine, gooseberries, and wild roses, like a fluffy candle-ring of green around a squatty brown candle. With each box I carried into the kitchen to unpack, I looked out the north window to the clearing where tall grass rippled in the wind.

Beyond the clearing, cottonwoods grew into a wood that hid within it a ditch and flume, dry now, used in spring to irrigate hay meadows to the east. The trees sheltered us from the world beyond, a buffer from sight and sound of traffic on the dirt road and the highway in the distance.

It seemed that everything had come together at last. Even though we hadn't yet achieved our own ranch dream, the cabin was surely the right place for us now. Our own world stretched out to the west, clusters of woods and pockets of tiny meadows laced with deer trails, noisy in the morning as magpies and squirrels quarreled in the treetops, quiet of evening save for a hurried rustle in the undergrowth and the gentle purr of the river.

The river was an entity, an everpresence like the air we breathed, a spare grandmother with flowing skirts to run to—one that always welcomed and soothed.

THERE'S FIRE SHOOTING
OUT THE CHIMNEY!

RIVER MUSIC HAS A RHYTHM, sometimes the fierce rush-and-tumble of a Beethoven finale, more often a *Clair-de-Lune* serenity. Either way, the rhythm worked its way under my skin into the drumbeat of my heart. The river's song settled me and linked me more deeply with the pulse of the land. I appreciated that and needed it to counterbalance the staccato chaos of these early days.

Inside the cabin, the mood was sometimes astringent. Toots had a new litter of kittens, and the abrupt removal of her nest-box from the tenant house to the cabin had left her rattled. I set up her nest behind the stove. She carried the kittens, one by one, onto Jenny's bed amid the stuffed animals, and then lovingly supplied them with freshly dead mice. The cat and I argued about this, and we finally compromised. I moved her nest-box into the bedroom by Jenny's bed. Toots agreed to the box's relocation but not to the culinary deprivation. I kept a sharp lookout for the mice.

Even Herbert was slow to settle in. Something was bothering him. I tried to explain that the large indoor population of rodents *should* bother a cat, but apparently I failed to strike the right chord. Striking any chord with Herbert was often difficult. I suspected that, like the cartoon Garfield, he and the mice chatted at night when the rest of us were in bed.

The paucity of cabinets and closets posed a challenge as to where to put stuff. For a while we lived out of cartons, clothesbaskets, and the two dressers we'd moved. We pawed through the boxes, extracted the essentials, then repacked and piled the boxes in corners or in the shed. Hopelessly Miscellaneous, which had never been opened since I'd packed it in Vermont, remained on the bottom of the stack. Over time, we put up hooks for hang-up clothes, shelves for books (one-by-sixes supported by stacks of Reader's Digest Condensed Books), and stuffed the leftovers into cheap, corrugated-board bins and cabinets.

The original sleeping arrangements for the kids became a point of contention, leading to complaints, tears, and arguments. Eventually, these evolved into a revolving system where beds changed inhabitants every few months, two kids in the bedroom, one on the living room couch, and one on the porch.

Right from the beginning, the kitchen and I squared off to do battle. With the stove in one corner and the pump diagonally opposite, no matter which one I dealt with, the other was at my back. They weren't about to succumb to quiet, obedient usefulness. But one of my first self-imposed chores was a paint job. I couldn't have survived those barf green walls for long. Real wainscoting it wasn't, but a strip of lath divided the walls into upper and lower halves. As soon as we could afford the paint, I covered the lower half with a light blue-green, the upper with white, coats and coats of white. Much better.

And Chuck had been right. As the days went by and I kept working the pump, the emerging syrup grew a shade lighter, a hair clearer, a bit more in quantity. The thought of ever drinking it, however—of actually serving it to my little family—was beyond the range of my imagination.

Meanwhile, the stove proved temperamental. Sometimes it worked beautifully, but shortly after we moved in, it decided to do an enthusiastic repeat of the smoke routine. Maybe the atmospheric pressure had something to do with its operation after all.

Smoke billowed. Toots came into the kitchen, looked around wildly, and dashed back to the bedroom. Seconds later, she reappeared with a small, gray, screeching ball of fur in her mouth. She ran to Peggy, who was lying in her appropriated spot by the stove, and dropped Willy between the dog's paws. (We always named the new kittens right away.) Willy started burrowing under Peggy, who jumped up and stared at him with furrowed brows. Nobody can look as worried as a German shepherd.

"Jenny," I said, "please grab Willy and take him and Peggy outside." This promised to be a long day—most of them were—but I planned to maintain cool control.

The boys turned up, and Toots dashed in with a calico kitten. She looked around for Peggy, and, distressed at not finding her, dropped Sunflower in the middle of the floor.

"Sam," I said, "would you please go get the other kittens before we're all nuts?"

Apparently overwhelmed by smoke, he gasped, clutched his throat, dropped to all fours, and crawled back to the bedroom, copied by Freddy who had trouble gasping and giggling at the same time.

"Frank, if you'll take Sunflower . . . "

"Don't need to," he said. Herbert plopped off a kitchen chair, picked up the stranded kitten with lethargic dignity, and carried it out. Frank and I followed. This kind of thing was all right in the summer, but I really hoped the stove and I would reach a more complete understanding before cold weather set in.

In a minute, Sam came around the back of the house, carrying the two remaining kittens. Freddy followed with the nest-box. Toots scooted along beside them, obviously pleased with her management of the situation. Of course they'd all gone out the window. Herbert had dropped Sunflower on the front steps, and now sat next to her, washing his face. No point in going any farther than necessary.

Standing in the yard, I pondered the smoke for a minute or two. Maybe it wasn't the atmospheric pressure after all. Maybe it was the kind of wood, or the way I laid the fire, or not enough kindling.

Peggy pressed against my knee, and I looked down. All four kittens seethed around her paws, and she looked up at me with enormous eyes, her brows even more furrowed than before. The boys had disappeared, and Toots was nowhere in sight. I sighed.

"I brought Sunflower over," Jenny said.

"Thank you," I said to Jenny and the dog both. "All right, let's fix up a place for now over in that shed." Carrying nest-box and kittens, we inspected the nearby structure. The roof and three walls seemed fairly tight for the most part, and the fourth side was open to the south. We found a secure and protected corner behind a piece of junk furniture and installed the kittens. Finding them would give Toots something to do. She might prefer living outside for a while anyway.

The stove gradually settled down and we went back in.

I saw the advantage of growing up with a woodstove: years of acclimating gradually to its tricks and vagaries rather than trying to learn it all at once. Maybe universities should offer Woodstove 101.

Learning to regulate the heat, especially for baking in the tight oven, tested my patience. The big heating stove in the living room accepted large, unsplit chunks of wood and lumps of coal when we could get them, which kept the fire burning for hours. But the kitchen cookstove needed smaller, split pieces that required frequent replenishing. What size pieces to use, whether to choose pine or cottonwood, how large a fire to build, how to keep the heat steady, how to manage the dampers to provide adequate draft but avoid chimney fires—in the end, the best teacher was experience. Eventually, the stove and I achieved a more or less agreeable working relationship.

I had to learn how often to dismantle and clean the stovepipe as well. Chimney fires were a hazard only when the soot buildup became too heavy. Once, early on, I heard a roaring in the pipe as it began to turn a glowing red. One of the kids flew into the kitchen to report, "There's fire shooting out the chimney!"

I called a neighbor who came over quickly with a ladder and something that looked like a green-glass ball but wasn't. He climbed on the roof and dropped the thing down the chimney. Whoosh! End of fire. I tried to get some (I never did find out what they consisted of) to have on hand, but found "they don't make 'em any more." Which was just as well, because the boys immediately wanted to climb on the roof and practice dropping things down the chimney.

I learned that the "front" of the stove was the side directly over the firebox (on the left), not the front we think of on an electric or gas stove. The "back" was the side farthest from the fire (to the right) and therefore a bit cooler. Since the stove had no burners, only a flat surface, I had to learn where to position a pot to get just the right heat. And I came to love the flexibility of this. Proper adjustment took only a shift two or three inches one way or the other.

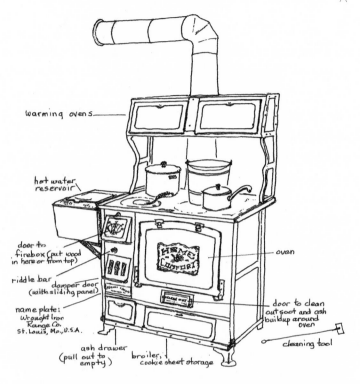

warming ovens

hot water reservoir

door to firebox (put wood in here or from top)

riddle bar
damper door (with sliding panel)

name plate:
Wrought Iron
Range Co.
St. Louis, Mo., U.S.A.

ash drawer
(pull out to empty)

broiler, cookie sheet storage

oven

door to clean out soot and ash buildup around oven

cleaning tool

As I say, this was a learn-by-experience skill. Attempting to make some chocolate fudge sauce one day to serve over ice cream, I lost concentration for a moment, and the pot boiled over. Wood-stove disadvantage: you can't just turn off the heat. The spill bubbled and burned, smoked and stank, clouding up the kitchen, until the burned chocolate finally formed a layer of crud. I used a spatula to scrape that off into the fire.

In contrast, the water reservoir presented a nice advantage. Attached to the stove next to the firebox, the storage tank gradually heated the water I poured into it, thereby keeping a supply of warm, though not boiling, water available.

The oven door formed part of the oven's temperature control. It opened in varying degrees—one-quarter inch, one-half inch—to cool the oven slightly if it got too hot. A damper at the back of the stove opened to let the heat from the firebox directly up the chimney (for quick stove-top cooking in summer), or closed to direct the heat around the oven (for baking). Adjusting the damper door on the front of the stove below the firebox allowed more or less air to fan the flames. A damper in the stovepipe under the warming ovens adjusted the draft. Beyond this welter of adjustments, a squarish "riddle bar" (heaven knows what the thing is officially called) stuck out from the front of the stove just below the firebox. By using a special tool (kind of a handle with a squarish, socket-type end), I could riddle, or rattle, the grates to let some ashes fall through into the ash drawer below, thereby increasing the amount of draft, which would make the fire burn hotter. Trying to coordinate all these settings made me feel like a one-woman three-ring circus until I got the knack. And of course, it all had to be constantly readjusted (or just the right amount and kind of wood added) to maintain the desired temperature. Emptying the ash drawer became another necessary chore.

The oven door closed with an extremely tight fit. Once, trying to produce Roy's favorite dessert, raisin pie, I got everything just right. I thought. With pleasure and satisfaction, I set the pie in on the shelf-rack (already adjusted to the right height, another learning point) to bake. I closed the door and felt accomplished. Peggy and I went outside to get in some wood, only to find the woodpile was nearly gone. We headed out to cut some more. Eventually we dragged back our harvest, and I started sawing. Some chunks needed splitting.

After a while, we returned to the house, and I replenished the fire. I remembered that I had a book review for a magazine due soon. Four hours later, after the kids came home, it occurred to me that I'd been doing something before going out for wood. Oh yes, making a pie for Roy.

A pie! I dashed to open the oven. Out rolled smoke and a burnt smell. The door fit so tightly that neither smell nor smoke had escaped earlier to give me warning. A hardened pie-sized disk slid out of its pan. I stabbed a knife into its middle and then carried it around, kind of like carrying a head on a pike. The kids laughed themselves silly. Even I thought it was pretty funny. They took the disk outside to play Frisbee until it disintegrated. I'm not sure I even told Roy about the nice surprise I'd planned for him.

And then there was Jenny's chocolate birthday cake. I was never sure exactly what happened there, but it didn't taste too bad as pudding with whipped cream. We had a birthday party anyway, although it was hard to keep the candles upright.

The warming ovens were the woodstove's glorious, totally trouble-free feature. Open, the doors presented an auxiliary work surface. Closed, the ovens warmed the dinner plates before serving time, or kept food hot, or hid and warmed baked goodies before revealing them for dessert. The joy of the warming ovens made up for a lot of the frustration with the rest of the stove.

The days began to take on something of a pattern. I always got up around five a.m., partly just to enjoy the quiet, but also to have a little uninterrupted time for some spiritual reading. I liked to gear myself up with good thoughts and verses to lean on throughout the day. I loved the beauty of the 139th Psalm: *If I take the wings of the morning, and dwell in the uttermost part of the sea; Even there shall thy hand lead me, and thy right hand shall hold me.* When I felt daunted and unsure of my ability to cope, this assurance of God's support boosted my courage.

If I'd gotten up early enough and the house was still quiet, I'd then settle to the joy of writing, something I'd loved ever since I was little. Maybe a poem, a story, or work on an article I hoped to sell, or at least give, to the local paper. When I was lucky, I'd get a few paragraphs written, even a page. Some days it didn't work out at all, but now in the cabin, this early-morning quiet time seemed more important to me than ever.

Often I wrote in my diary, a red, hardcover Daily Reminder, sometimes recording the happenings of the last day or two, complete with dialog. Or I wrote about the land, the weather, the river, the animals, trying, somehow, to describe the world of nature that surrounded me. If I had a specific project in progress, an article for the newspaper perhaps, of course I'd work on that.

About this time, I read in a writers' magazine that you could write a novel in a year, working just half an hour a day. Okay, I tried that, and stretching the time into eighteen months or so, I *did* complete a novel. The article hadn't guaranteed that the tome would be any good—mine was awful—but I proved to myself that I really could start a book and write to the finish.

I'd loved to write from the time I first learned to print block letters. On my first day of kindergarten, to show off my prowess with words, I signed my crayoned masterpiece (stripe of blue sky at the top, stripe of green grass at the bottom, house and stick-person me in the middle) with the word, "HAM." We'd had ham for supper the night before.

My grade school literary works impressed my mother so much, she started saving whatever money she could scrape together (those were tough times, the final years of World War II) to buy me a typewriter for my sixth-grade graduation, which coincided with my twelfth birthday. My own typewriter! I continued to prize my Smith-Corona portable through high school and college and into marriage. I still have it. With the typewriter came an instruction book, and that summer I spent unreasonable amounts of time in my room, teaching myself to type, a skill that proved useful over the years.

For me, one of the best things about moving to the cabin was its proximity to the big house where Ellie lived. Both buildings were part of the same ranchstead. While well separated by fences, dooryard, and barn, they were close enough to walk easily between the two. Ellie and I had already been working together on her series of horse training articles, and now we could spend more time with the project.

Along with raising and showing Arabian horses and German shepherd dogs, Ellie trained horses for others, taught riding classes for the University of Wyoming, gave private lessons, and managed her eight-week summer horsemanship school. She ended up mimeographing, later photocopying, a lot of material for her various classes and wished she could find a textbook that contained all the information she wanted her students to study.

Finally it occurred to us that Ellie could write her own book. She'd been an art major in college, and our various talents jibed perfectly. She could illustrate horse tack, dressage and reining patterns, anatomy, and so on with clear line drawings. I would photograph her training techniques. I could supplement her first draft with ideas gleaned from the library of horse books I was accumulating. Eventually this developed into a workable system. She wrote a first draft on yellow legal pads. I'd organize, edit, and type it up. She'd go over and edit. I'd retype. I bought reams of cheap, yellow "second sheets" or newsprint to use until the final draft. Sometimes a chapter or section would make a lot of trips back and forth.

While Ellie was the expert on content for her textbook, I was supposedly the expert on writing. I had a tenuous knowledge of only one major publisher, and that because I'd grown up in Garden City, New York, then home to Doubleday Doran. This publishing facility, a mile or so from our home, had its own station, Country Life Press, on a branch line of the Long Island Rail Road

Since neither Ellie nor I had even heard of a "book proposal," we struggled along, chapter by chapter, fitting writing time into the crannies left by our other activities. Eventually, after a couple of years, stacks of legal pads, and reams and reams of paper, we had five or six chapters. Now we could see that our original plan for a book covering riding, training, and all aspects of horse care would probably run to three or four thousand pages. We amended our outline into a whole series of books. So now what?

Doubleday, of course. But how to contact them? Simple. My parents still lived in Garden City. I sent them the manuscript and asked my mother to take it over to the Doubleday building. No problem. Ever supportive, she did just that. First snag: the huge complex only printed and shipped books. The editorial offices were in New York City. Faithfully, she hauled the manuscript into Manhattan.

Either she was even more determined and resourceful than I'd realized, or maybe it's just that we were favored by beginner's luck. At any rate, the manuscript eventually found its way to senior editor Ellin K. Roberts, who worked with horse books including such brilliant and notable author / rider / trainers as Alois Podhajsky, former director of the Spanish

Riding School of Vienna, and William Steinkraus, captain of the United States Equestrian Olympic Team. Ellin rejected our manuscript in the nicest possible way ("This decision is based entirely on the fact that between the books we have already published in this field and further projects already under contract . . . etc."). But she offered crumbs of comfort ("Your prospectus for a series of books on riding, and the sample chapters and outline for the first volume certainly suggest that you have a wealth of sound, practical advice to contribute.") and the beautiful suggestion to submit the material to William Steinkraus. He was now an editor at Van Nostrand, building a list of books on the equestrian arts. This time we mailed the manuscript instead of pressing my mother into another trip into New York City for hand delivery.

About a month later, my father died suddenly, and I made my way back to Long Island. He had supported my writing and always encouraged me to take advantage of any opportunity. Although the occasion was sad, I knew he'd want me to go ahead with meeting an editor if I could. When would I ever have another chance to get back to New York? So after the funeral, I decided to call Mr. Steinkraus and see if he'd looked at the manuscript. He told me he'd see me early the next morning.

Bill Steinkraus rejected the book, but he gave me an hour of critique and suggestions. "Refocus on addressing basic horsemanship as a basis for *both* English and Western riding: no one else has done that. Include more photos and illustrations; they will help sell the book." And best of all: "Try me again."

So Ellie and I went back to the drawing board, revising our outline and the chapters we'd already written, and writing more. We never guessed how many more years we'd be working on this project or even imagined the glitches that could occur in the world of publishing. Meanwhile, life bustled on.

HOW COME YOU DIDN'T
LIGHT THE FIRE?

ROY AND THE KIDS SETTLED in to our new way of life more quickly than I did. The adjustments I had to make in my daily pattern of living seemed overwhelming. Everything depended on something else. A cup of coffee? I had no percolator, and since Roy didn't drink coffee anyway, I used only instant. But this still required boiling the river water in the kettle, which required getting the water from the river and starting a fire in the stove, which required having kindling and wood, which required filling the woodbox, which required having pieces of wood, which required chopping, which required sawing logs into stove-lengths to chop, which required hauling in logs to saw.

I had to begin thinking ahead. I made sure the kids dipped pails of water from the river in the evening, to fill the teakettle and prime the pump at dawn. We kept flashlight batteries on hand so we weren't plunged into darkness on the way to the privy. Once we lost a flashlight that had been set down carelessly in the outhouse and rolled off the seat into the depths, glowing eerily below for some hours. After a while we used kerosene lanterns that we could set firmly on the privy seat, which meant remembering to buy kerosene.

I planned food for the day that I could cook in the morning, making potato salad or stew or spaghetti that could be easily reheated in the electric fry pan. A microwave oven would have been a welcome miracle, but if they had come into use then, we wouldn't have known about them. We ate a lot of peanut butter and jelly sandwiches, fortunately one of Roy's favorite foods.

In warm weather, the river served as our bathtub, and this worked beautifully. Apparently for kids, there's a remarkable difference between climbing into a tub to be scrubbed and trying to keep track of a bar of Ivory in a sun-warmed river backwater. For myself, considering the possibilities of interruption, I generally opted for sponge baths.

Once the weather cooled, we resorted to washing in "The Tub," a two-by-four-foot stock tank Roy had picked up at an auction. We hauled it in by the stove to warm up a bit. We stoked up the fire, heated buckets and buckets of water, poured them into tub, tested water with finger, added more hot or cold—then the cleanest (least dirty) kids got in first. The younger kids could stretch out their legs, but the older ones had to keep knees bent. I wanted to take a picture of Roy bathing, but he didn't cotton to the idea. The nasty part was dipping out the dirty water into buckets to dump outside until the water was low enough that Roy and I could carry the tub outside to dump the rest.

Washing dishes wasn't too difficult, once I got the hang of it. I heated water in a bucket on the stove and poured that into a pot large enough to immerse the dinner plates, while heating more water in buckets and the teakettle. I put a small drainboard on the miniscule counter, set the soapy dishes into the rack, and rinsed them by pouring boiling water over them. And yes, after dark I lit the kerosene lamp that I'd set on the corner shelf above the sink, better lighting than the bulb in the center of the ceiling (now sixty watts, instead of the original fifteen), which threw my own shadow across whatever I was doing. The trick was not to let dirty dishes accumulate, in which case, they'd have to be piled on the table and cleared a few at a time.

With the lack of counter space, the mustard-yellow kitchen table became the Center of All Things, especially of food preparation. We ate there, of course, and it also served as a desk for me and for Roy; a place for kids to do their homework; a place to work on hobbies such as bug collections, a place for mail, flashlights, magazines, and groceries that didn't fit in the cabinets, such as constantly-used jars of peanut butter; a place to put all the stuff I cleared off of it in the morning and put on the bed, which had to be cleared off at night so Roy and I could sleep. The table was hard to clean, considering all the stuff that kept turning up on it, although once I thought about it, items like last night's empty pickle jar could simply be thrown away. And then there were the dirty dishes along with a variety of inherited silverware (family leftovers: nothing matched), and vestiges of egg or ketchup. Someday I still must find time to investigate the magnetic properties of mustard-yellow Formica.

The essential chore for all of us came down to procuring wood for the stoves. We acquired a firewood permit to cut in the Medicine Bow National Forest. Roy would take a boy or two and they'd go to the mountains to fill the pickup with stove-length chunks (eventually he bought a chainsaw) to split later at home with ax or splitting maul. Sometimes we'd all cram into the pickup (Peggy and picnic lunch included) to spend the day, which was probably less efficient than it should have been, since it amounted to a lot of playing around in the woods. When we acquired a twenty-year-old two-ton truck, we could haul more wood at a time.

After haying season, when ranch work slowed, Roy began to worry more about our finances. His dreams of building a ranching empire kept spinning away at an ever-faster rate, and he began to lose something of his freewheeling nature. But that didn't speed him up. If anything, it weighed on him and slowed him down even more. Just keeping up with the present had become a problem, let alone worrying about the future. He wrote me in a note:

> *Dear Sweet Little Gayseypuss, Yesterday I had the best day I've had in a long time. I got many things done (correctly done). Today I'm going to have to get on the ball, or I'll be back in my old slump of 10 days ago, or so.*

Roy got a job in Laramie with the Railway Express Agency, which wasn't part of the railroad companies, but operated in conjunction with them. The Union Pacific ran a lot of trains through Laramie, and for a while, the Railroad Post Office (RPO) cars still operated. Bags of letters, direct from the post office, would be sorted as the train traveled, resulting in speedy delivery across the country.

Roy's heart was in ranching, and he wasn't fond of either the long commute or the type of work, but it paid the bills. And, since he'd always enjoyed steam engines, especially the Big Boys (the huge 4000 series), he loved hearing the huffing steam, the slip and rumble of the wheels, the wail of the whistles.

The downside of the Railroad Express Agency job hit rock bottom when new management came up with some "bright ideas" intended to attract more business. Immediately obvious to local employees was the fact that while the new

CEOs may have been skilled and experienced in administration and management, they were totally at sea when it came to the practical workings of the company. Part of Roy's job consisted of sorting the freight that came in and then delivering shipments and packages to stores and offices in town. When one new directive arrived from the head office, it was accompanied by a bag of fake silver bullets. The instructions were to deliver the package, leave a bullet beside it, then dash out of the store shouting, "R-E-A-Awa-a-a-ay!" Even the Lone Ranger would have been appalled. This was intended to impress customers with the speed, efficiency, and perhaps ubiquity of REA deliveries. Rather, it impressed the employees that management had slipped a cog, and they rebelled in disgust at the absurdity.

Roy couldn't even imagine himself scattering silver bullets around, much less pulling off such antics. But I enjoyed imagining. While chopping wood or resting by the river, I envisioned Roy in a mask, tucking a bullet surreptitiously under the edge of a package and sprinting to the front of the store, then turning, his hand raised in a sweeping gesture, as he sang out the signature cry. For a while silver bullets became popular kids' toys in the area.

I helped earn a little where I could. Through our tenuous connection with the university, I ended up typing papers for Afghan, Iranian, and other foreign students, this for real money instead of trade. Their English was certainly far better than my non-existent Pushtu or whatever, but still, between their written instructions and oral elucidations, communication was a challenge. I *worked* for the coins that were forthcoming. If I'd added my time into the equation, I'd have been paying for the privilege of typing. I wrote my parents about one early experience with this, and my mother kept a letter that noted my difficulties with "the structure of periclinal chimeras, the homologous nature of the non-homologous meiotic pairing in Triticum stivum deficient for chromosome V (5B)," and similar phrases.

I was using my old Smith-Corona for this, and while it continued to function, it was getting tired (possibly of the big words). Also, the font was pica, and the academic preference seemed to be for the smaller elite type, probably because with more words to a page, it was cheaper for them. Roy found an elegant old Underwood, the kind that weighed a ton and sat like a throne on the table. It had nice action and a particularly pretty bell that rang at the end of each line, alerting me to hit the carriage-return lever with my left pinky. Its font was elite.

I helped with housecleaning and lawn work around the neighborhood, and with special projects such as painting and washing walls and ceilings. From our earliest married days, Roy had wanted me to cut his hair and was willing to put up with jagged beginning efforts. And so I cut the kids' hair, too, and next thing I knew, I was asked to cut hair for the neighbors (Not for money. I certainly didn't want to run into trouble with a barbers' union, if there was one). This also brought an exchange—most often firewood, or sometimes coal (great for keeping the big "acorn" stove going in the living room), all of which was much appreciated.

When ranchers were short-handed, I'd fill in driving a tractor with rake in the hayfield, or with livestock work (such as manning the squeeze chute for pregnancy testing cows, dehorning, or vaccinating calves), or with winter feeding. This sometimes paid around a dollar an hour. Branding, of course, was a neighboring thing. I helped in kitchen or corral or wherever needed. Around here, "neighbor" was a verb, and I frequently neighbored.

But none of this made much of an impact on our finances. Our mail always seemed to be laced with bills. One night Roy and I were discussing a compulsory socialized medicine bill that President Johnson had signed that day. I told him about one report I'd heard: "Johnson used seventy-two pens to sign the bill."

The kids were supposed to be asleep, but then Sam called from the bedroom, "Did Johnson send us a bill?"

Our main concern continued to revolve around keeping the woodboxes full. Because the busy activity at the REA depot required attendants to be on hand around the clock, Roy often worked the night shift or sometimes double shifts. He tried to keep wood available for us, but sometimes we'd run low. Occasionally we were able to buy a load of firewood, or more often, trade with neighbors for labor of some kind.

In any case, plenty of trees surrounded our home, and I

could handle these myself, if need be. Thick growth crowded out a lot of the cottonwoods along the ditchbanks and back in the woods, and some trees died early, their trunks only four to five inches across. With my bow-saw and the dog for a helper, I'd enjoy a walk in the woods, pick a likely tree, and plan my strategy. If I wanted the tree to fall that way, I started sawing here and made a small notch. Then I'd saw from the other side until the tree toppled, sometimes right where I'd planned. I got pretty good at felling trees.

Peggy cheered me on, standing back to watch the top of the tree as it swayed, and barking in jubilant anticipation of the crash. When it fell, she rushed in to rip off the dead bark and any small limbs that hadn't broken away. After trimming off the remaining branches, I'd drag home our prize. Peggy helped by carrying the small end of the tree, the only trouble being that she trotted along faster than I, swinging the tree around so that we proceeded in a scallop pattern along the trail. Roy or the boys sawed our bounty into firewood when they got home from work or school. Sometimes Roy set out a kerosene lantern and split wood after dark.

On one of those early mornings in the cabin, I pulled on Levi's and sweatshirt, then started to light a fire in the stove. I tried to lay the fire the night before, so it would be ready to spring alive at the strike of a match, but this time I'd forgotten. I wadded up some newspaper, popped it into the firebox, reached for some kindling, looked into an empty box. The kids forgot to bring in the kindling. Hoping the fire might start anyway, I laid two split pieces of wood on the paper, struck a match, and watched a flame flare up.

Then I crossed the kitchen diagonally to pour a dipper or two of water into the pump. We kept a pail of river water by the door, anticipating the pump's lack of cooperation. It should have held its prime, but hadn't so far (and never did). Forever optimistic, I hoped for clear, pristine drinking water. I banged the handle up and down furiously and added more water and said unpleasant things under my breath. Thus persuaded, the pump finally caught, complained bitterly, and sprayed out a tired mass of watery moss and spider legs. Not just the thing at 5:10 in the morning, but better than before. Reeling a little, I pumped it dry, now taking a little longer, and told it where to go. It hissed back at me.

I filled the teakettle with river water from the pail. This looked pretty good, but I'd heard about all the terrible things floating around in crystal mountain streams, so I boiled the water thoroughly before drinking. All right, so I'd have to wait half an hour for my coffee. I put the teakettle on the stove.

The fire was out.

A fierce banging shook the kitchen window. Probably Toots, since the cats were now spending the nights outside. I ignored it.

I stuck my head into the bedroom and sang out, "Roy, dear, time to get up." He was better at fires than I was, even though he hadn't had much more experience with them, beyond his Boy Scout days. Maybe he was just slow and careful enough to arrange the kindling exactly right before striking the match.

The dog yawned and stretched, and that was all the response I got. Further banging on the kitchen window ensued, enough to rattle the light fixture, but not enough to disturb Roy. "Cut it out, you old bat," I yelled from the bedroom. Maybe the combined noise would wake Roy. No luck. More banging. Tell a cat to cut it out and see where you get. She'd learned the trick accidentally—at least I think it was accidental—when she scratched her ear with her hind leg, and her hock hit the glass with staccato reverberations. Now, to attract attention, she positioned herself properly and scratched her ear.

Peggy trotted past me out of the bedroom. I saw her go to the window and grin at Toots. *Hee hee, you're out and I'm inside.*

Back to the problem at hand. "Roy, wake up! Time to go to work!" Still no response. He was hanging off the far side of the bed, and I couldn't reach him easily or I'd have punched him one. Peggy returned to the bedroom and started her "I have to go out" routine, kind of a Fred Astaire tap dance with four feet at once, clickety-clickety-click with the toenails, accompanied by a lot of head-tossing and guttural comments that increased in intensity as they increased in duration. Toots observed the beginnings of the dance and acknowledged its efficacy; she disappeared from the window, probably to pry at the door with her claws.

Peggy and I crossed the porch without turning on the light, a potentially dangerous maneuver considering the stuff we still had piled all over. The light cord dangled from the ceiling somewhere. To fish for it in the dark was as hazardous as doing without the light. Opening the front door, with the cat poised to come in and the dog dancing to go out, required strategy to avoid getting knocked down in the two-way rush. I tripped over the antique cream separator (important parts missing) that stood for some reason by the door, probably because it had never been moved elsewhere, and nudged the dog south, thereby clearing a mini-channel to the north for the cat, if I could open the door fast enough. This worked, and the switch was made. However, the pail that some nitwit had balanced on the separator fell off into the small stock tank we used as a bathtub. A bit of a racket.

Again back to the bedroom. The pump hissed at me as I went by. Roy was still dead to the world. "Roy, wake up! It's getting late!" I leaned across the bed, one knee heavy on the mattress near the headboard—BAM! With a bone-jarring crunch, the bedsprings hit the floor, the head end of the mattress dropped, and the foot end went up.

"Huzzah whazuzzah," Roy yelled, flailing around. "Lyndon Baines Johnson! Whatcha convention! Whaza Democrats doing now!"

"Damn," I said, extricating myself. "I forgot to check those bed slats. Anyway, it's time to get up."

"Oops," he said, apparently awake now.

"What?"

"*Oops.* You *should* have said 'oops'." He was lying there at a forty-five-degree angle, feet up, making exaggerated motions with his eyebrows and shaking his head violently, presumably to indicate the presence of young ears beyond thin walls.

"H-E-double toothpicks!" I said with some emphasis. "Your face is getting red."

"En garde!" The shout came from behind me. Sam stood there in his shorts with a baseball bat in one hand and a big pot lid in the other, stabbing around with the bat and then leaping into a crouch.

"Whasamatter with you!" I yelled. This was my second yell, or maybe third, and it wasn't 5:30 yet. "What're you up for, anyway?"

He straightened and smiled sweetly. "Ah yes! What'm I up for? Machine gun fire at the kitchen window, cannonading in the shed, bombs bursting in the bedroom! I am here to lend assistance. I seek to serve by wallowing into the fray . . . ."

"Beat it, you crackpot," I said. You're probably not supposed to address your children that way, but I didn't think of it at the time.

Suddenly I realized that my little trip down the primrose path was somewhat overdue. I was only too happy to leave the bedroom.

Outside, the carnival atmosphere of the cabin dissolved. Dawn fingered the sky, shooting a rosy glow into the gray.

The river murmured and slapped and, with a thunderous patter of paws, Peggy galloped up to greet me as though I'd been gone for two months. Over by one of the sheds, a bunny hopped and nibbled. A horse's nicker blew in on a gentle wisp of clean-smelling breeze. Birds swung into full crescendo after an earlier tune-up, and a sleepy-eyed Herbert, washing his face in the doorway of the kids' tree house, paused to contemplate the sky.

Maybe it was all worthwhile after all.

However, when I forgot to duck under the willow branch, I wasn't so sure. With only the dog to hear, I said "damn" quite loudly and repeated it several times with a variety of tone and emphasis.

By the time I got back to the cabin a few minutes later, with my eyes still watering, Roy had the fire roaring away in the stove, and the teakettle was on its way to a twenty-minute boil. The pump remained quiet and innocent. Toots was purring.

"Traitors," I muttered.

Roy said, "How come you didn't light the fire earlier?"

HOWDY, NEIGHBOR!

G RADUALLY, LIVING IN THE CABIN LOST its element of novelty. Everyday tasks became routine. While my body went through the motions of pumping water or contending with the stove, I could think about my writing projects, or consider the kids' progress in school, or prepare for upcoming meetings. Occasionally I'd find myself reflecting on the nature of this place where we'd chosen to live.

The ranching communities of the Laramie plains presented a far different lifestyle from the neighborhoods where Roy and I grew up. We'd both been raised in big-city suburbs, with their grid of roads and squarish blocks sectioned into 60 by 100-foot plots. Our homes each faced the street. A path ran from front door to sidewalk, and the back door opened only to family, tradesmen, and the closest of backyard friends.

Here, ranchsteads stretched like mile-spaced beads along the Laramie River and its main artery, the Pioneer Canal. The school, instead of being "a couple of streets over," represented a hub, its radii extending miles in every direction.

In the suburbs, most of the men commuted to the big city where their jobs or professions varied with each individual. The women stayed home, took care of children and household tasks, and budgeted the dollars allotted to them by the bread-winner. We kids, compact groups of blockmates, played soft-ball, catch, or square dodgeball in the street, all within call of home. Adult conversation centered on news and business, Brooklyn Dodgers versus the Yankees, grocery-store sales, and small economies. Except during World War II, few people raised a garden.

Here in ranch country, conversation centered on water and weather. Was the drought local or widespread? Should we sell down the cattle now or wait? Do we have enough hay to carry us over if it's a hard winter? The river was an umbilical cord of life-giving water that focused everyone's attention on their common livelihood. Everyone gardened and canned and dried and preserved, in partnership with, or sometimes in deep struggle with, the whims of nature and the land.

I'd always been drawn to the land. As a child, I'd take our beagle, Nibsy, on walks to the "Lots," where grass and weeds grew undisturbed, and where we'd scare up an occa-sional rabbit, to the little dog's delight. Later, I rode my bike on weekends, alone or with friends, through the winding country roads of the island's north shore. I'd stop to visit horses pastured near the woodsy roads and imagined foxes beyond the hedgerows. And I read voraciously, especially of the wild freedoms of the West, gradually narrowing my interest down to Wyoming.

And now I was here. Somehow the dream had turned into reality. As far as my feelings about the land were concerned, I'd finally "come home." But socially I felt out of place, although the kids didn't seem hobbled or even touched by the outlander perceptions that hovered in the back of my mind. I think Roy might have felt as I did, though he would never admit it. He quickly adopted the local vernacular and dialect, correcting me when I slipped into an eastern pronunciation and said, for instance, Nevahda or Colorahdo, instead of pronouncing the *a's* as in "hat."

Rural communities tend to be close-knit, especially when families have been living in the same place "unto the third and fourth generation," those generations having established a homogenous and traditional way of life. Trying to weave one's own life-strands into the tight fabric, rather than just embroider them over the top, can be tough.

Here families socialized together. I was impressed by and grateful for the local emphasis on kids, the pride and care rural people took in family and in nourishing the upcoming generation, imparting competence, tradition, and the ability to cope with life itself. This was something Roy and I wanted for our own kids, the development of a work ethic that fostered confidence and capability. We embraced the notion of all members of the family working together toward a common goal instead of fragmenting into separate spheres, not always even coming together for supper in the evening. Suburban children were often unaware, and perhaps didn't care, what kept Pop away from home all day, what provided the food and clothing and house they lived in.

I surprised myself by realizing how much I'd adopted this new mindset when talking with a well-to-do family who had just bought a ranch down the river to the east. They had two kids about the same age as ours. Right to begin with, the parents asked: "What other couples our own age do you get together with around here?" *Our own age?* They expected to continue the stratified social engagement they'd come from, and I had trouble explaining the fine mix of grandparents, parents, teenagers, kids and babies, and even the peripheral Benny, the bachelor rancher who sat among the kids for school movies.

Nevertheless, I often felt awkward, like the new kid on the block or perhaps the ragged stepchild, not altogether belonging, only renting, not owning—until I had occasion to visit our next-door neighbors to the west, a family who had lived there for generations. I'm sure Roy, the kids, and I had been there before, probably for 4-H meetings, but this time I was alone. I drove up near the back door, the main door of nearly all country houses, in contrast to urban custom. The back door entered the kitchen, the heart of the home. In many cases, the front door, the formal entrance into a hallway or parlor, had no pathway leading to it or even remained inaccessible.

I'd been painfully shy as a child, sometimes hiding under the dining room table when my mother had company, much to her embarrassment. I still found myself uncertain when in unfamiliar territory. For one thing, I didn't want to bother people or interrupt them if they were doing something important or push myself where I might not be wanted.

I parked and pondered how I'd have to cross the yard to the steps of this neighbor's house, knock on the door, and (trained by my mother never to try to peer into someone's house) then stare out across the fields and river to Jelm Mountain, waiting for someone to come, wondering if I'd caught them at a bad moment, wondering . . . .

But even before I climbed out of the pickup, Margaret threw open the back door, beamed on me from the stoop, held out her arms, and called "Howdy, neighbor!" The cloak of warmth and welcome flew out, settled over me, and gathered me in. Today I still get all tingly thinking about it.

Others who gathered us in included Conrad and Dena Hansen, an elderly couple who lived several miles upriver, just above Woods Landing, where Woods Creek cut through the mountains to join the Laramie River. Woods Landing had grown at the junction of highways 230 and 10, where a bridge crossed the Laramie River. Not so much a community as a gathering place, the Landing had sprouted a combination bar, tiny store with an old metal Wonderbread sign on the door, and sometime post office (Jelm—the site of the post office moved from place to place, depending on its current postmaster). Most significantly, a large dance hall had been built there, which hosted festivities of all kinds.

I first met Connie in a grocery store in Laramie. Thin, a little stooped, he wore his signature blue hard hat with "Hansen" printed on the brim. Always interested in local history, I'd been researching an old ghost town, Cummins City, up the river from Woods Landing. Someone told me to see Conrad Hansen, who knew a lot about the area. When I saw the name on his hat, I approached him and introduced myself. He was filling his cart with jars of honey. He turned on me a huge grin and the brightest eyes I'd ever seen and launched into friendly conversation.

"I'm buying honey for my bees."

"*For* the bees?" I asked, surprised.

Evidently just the response he'd hoped for! It set him off on an explanation of how his bees needed food. Spring had been late after a tough winter, and the alfalfa was slow to bloom. The bees needed to build up their strength until they could forage on their own. Eventually we got around to the topic of Cummins City, and Connie invited us to his ranch, upriver from us, but just down the river from the ghost town. He had lived on the little ranch since the early 1900s. Its hay meadows hugged the river along the narrow valley between Jelm Mountain to the east and the steep foothills and canyons of the Medicine Bow Mountains to the west.

Connie and Dena welcomed us like family, and before long, we visited back and forth frequently. They became surrogate grandparents to our kids.

Connie loved telling about the past. He'd set up his own museum on his ranch, with artifacts from an earlier era—tools and lamps, arrowheads and animal skulls, kitchen utensils and antique gadgets of all sorts—and each one held a story. He reveled in history, especially hands-on, and took us to see the sites of old mines and graves, the remains of one of the great Indian (possibly pre-Indian?) seasonal migration trails, and of course, Cummins City.

One day, with Sam, Frank, and me, he turned off the highway onto a dirt road that faded into the rangeland. We crossed a narrow wooden bridge over the Laramie River and followed the road south, past remains of cabins and piles of weathered boards. We passed a compact log structure with a small steeple. It appeared intact.

"That looks like a church." Frank said,

"Church and school both, for a while. Not many cabins left now."

As we bounced along, he told us how John Cummins, an enterprising Denverite, salted a few small mines in the area back around 1880.

"Cummins selected some shiny ore samples, flashed them around in town, and dropped hints about rich deposits. In no time, people piled into the valley, set up tents and built cabins. Somebody erected a steam sawmill to make lumber."

Sam wondered about the sawmill, and Connie said, "I'll show you the remains of that."

He parked and we piled out. Gathering a surveyor's chain, transit, and stakes, Connie bounded off to measure foundations and distances, trailed by the boys, while I stumbled along through the sagebrush, taking notes and trying not to miss anything. He explained the surveying process, which for me went in one ear and out the other while I concentrated on history and story. The boys dashed around in Connie's wake, holding chain or stakes, and obviously having a great time.

"Cummins did a good job of propaganda," Connie said. "By 1881, the mining camp was known as Cummins City."

Later I found an article in the *Laramie Sentinel,* March 29, 1881, that reported the town "now has thirty-one houses occupied, four saloons and four stores, all of which are doing a rushing business." It said, too, that a 60 by 100-foot hotel was under construction. Connie found the foundations that remained, and he and the boys measured it off. "Folks said it had forty rooms, but I think even twenty would be a stretch."

In April 1881, another *Sentinel* article reported the existence of over a hundred houses along with a Sabbath school building. Humorist Bill Nye lived there for a while and wrote some of his stories from Cummins City. Mining companies moved in, stock sold well, and soon four doctors, along with lawyers, a judge, and other professional men, moved out from Laramie to settle in the thriving community.

"I remember hearing stories about how folks could just scrape up dirt from their cabin floors and pan enough gold out of it to make a profit. Rumor was such fun, nobody paid any attention to the truth."

But eventually the truth won out, people up and left, and the town withered as fast as it had bloomed. Connie said, "John Cummins went on a business trip to Denver, and I reckon he's still there on business. At least he never came back. Some folks lived on for a while, and the name was changed to Jelm. Maybe they just wanted to forget about John Cummins, but the hotel disappeared pretty quick. Ranchers and other folks used the lumber for their own buildings."

Connie and Dena usually seemed at odds with each other, bantering in a way that kept the kids laughing, although I sometimes wondered if it was really as good-natured as it seemed. "We agree some of the time," Dena said, "but most of the time, we don't." But then, she was Swedish, Connie Norwegian. She consumed cases of Pepsi and astounded Roy by watching TV, reading a book, and carrying on a conversation all at once, apparently without losing track of a single word in any of them.

Dena enjoyed feeding us, especially since the kids had pretty much all arrived at the bottomless-pit stage. Her mulligan stew was a favorite, and she often brought a big pot when she and Connie came to visit us at the cabin. At her house she sometimes made Swedish *krumkaker*, patterned pancakes that she twisted into cones and filled with a cream concoction. Her "dip" became a favorite with the kids. The sweet sauce, made by boiling water, cornstarch, sugar, and vanilla, could be poured over even stale cake or biscuits, immediately transforming the original into a fabulous dessert. Except once.

The kids and I had gone over one Sunday afternoon when Roy was working. I'd been encouraging Connie to write some of his stories and needed to collect his papers to type them up. Dena whipped up some dip (the kids had to have their special treat) then slathered it on day-old chocolate cake. The kids dug in as usual. But then they began picking at the dessert. Connie, Dena, and I were discussing some historical oddity until Dena looked over at the table.

"Eat up," she enthused. "Here, have some more dip?"

Frank shook his head. Sam said, "No, this is fine," and Jenny and Freddy looked worried. Sam tried pushing the dip to the side and concentrating on the cake. They all dawdled but kept eating. Slowly. By this time, I too had some cake and dip and finally dug in myself.

"Hmmm," I said. "Um, Dena, this seems a little off."

"Why? What's the matter?" She ran a finger along the edge of the pot and licked it. "Oh my stars!"

"Trying to poison the company," Connie said. "I might have guessed you'd get around to it." He hadn't had any.

For once she ignored him. "Don't eat any more!" She whisked away the kids' dishes, dumped their cake into the garbage, and launched into a tirade while Connie chuckled or maybe cackled. "Don't ever do that again!" she roared at the kids. "You don't have to be polite around here! Don't eat it. Just *tell* me if it's no good!" She dumped the pot of dip down the drain, grabbed canisters off the shelf, clattered dishes and pans. "I used the wrong canister by mistake, salt instead of sugar. Here, wash it down with Pepsi. I'll start over."

She turned to me, still fuming. "Teaching kids to be polite is one thing, but this is ridiculous!" Connie was still cackling, and by this time, I was pretty close to it myself. But actually, I was proud of them. Maybe they *were* carrying politeness too far on this occasion, but better that than some of the responses I could imagine. Now they sat wide-eyed, trying to figure out whether it was funny or not. But then Dena laughed at herself, and before long, we finished up the cake with real dip while Connie got out his violin. Even with arthritic fingers, he could set the room rocking with the old fiddle, and we all tapped toes along with him.

At home we got used to making our trips to the privy when the weather was fine, but never quite delighted in the journey when it rained or the path crunched with cold. Roy sawed off the willow branch, which raised my spirits considerably. Jenny hated the trip and at night imagined the trail strewn with snakes. She needed my company. The path soon assumed a well-trodden look while the privy seat itself acquired a renewed polish. Of course, the walk, though short, could be adventurous, especially at night when the lantern sent giant-leg shadows dancing through the bushes. When the smell of skunk scented the air, we proceeded cautiously.

And one night Frank called in alarm, "Ma, there's a porcupine on the path to the privy!" I joined him and we followed slowly as the ball of quills lumbered along the trail and out of our way.

Eventually, the pump cooperated enough that we didn't have to haul water from the river, and by the time six months had passed, it even looked like good clear water. In a letter to my parents, I reported, "Took a water sample in to be tested— still waiting to hear if it's deadly poison or purity itself. Maybe they gave it the taste test and nobody lived to make a report." When the report finally came in, it showed the water was okay to drink.

Dawn usually kicked off the day with a flourish. The birds called it into being, the sky lightened with anticipation, then brightened with expectation, and finally exploded into joyous color. At last the sun tipped the mountains and then spilled out over the valley. I was glad the necessary privy trip pulled me outside so I wouldn't miss the show. Sometimes I'd step a little ways north into the clearing to get a better view of Sheep Mountain to the northwest, polished gold with sunrise. How could anyone bear to miss the excitement of such an extraordinary event, presented free of charge, requiring only our attention and gratitude?

In contrast, the evenings held their own essence of peace, a letting-go of the tensions and insistences of the day as the sun melted down behind the mountains and spread a lavender glow across the landscape. Deer drifted into the yard, grazing their way to drink at the river. Coyotes sang in harmony beyond the ridge to the south.

Occasionally, Roy called us all out in the middle of the night to watch a meteor shower and count the falling stars, to admire the Northern Lights or the Milky Way, or to study a lunar eclipse. Once, when a great horned owl hooted nearby, we all ran out to see. Sitting on the top branch of a cottonwood by the house, he called, deep-throated and eerie. Another owl answered from across the river. Spellbound, we felt shivers up our spines. Our owl hooted again, spread his wings, drifted to another tree, then disappeared into night.

ARE YOU REALLY
MOVING TO BORNEO?

W HEN THE THREE OLDER KIDS hopped into the little
yellow school bus that first fall after we moved to the
cabin, Fred (now grown out of the nickname Freddy) played
with Peggy in the yard, or he climbed into the tree house, or
helped me get wood or bake cookies. Sometimes Fred, Peggy,
and I would go to town to buy groceries or wash clothes at
the laundromat, or whatever else was on the agenda. And always we stopped at the library.

At home, we often ran down the path to the river, where
Fred and Peggy played in the water while I sat back on the
grassy bank. Peggy had become an indispensable part of the
family, a loyal companion for me and a friend and guardian
for Fred and the other kids. She was intelligent and quick to
catch on. We invented a workable game of softball with the
kids as one team, Peggy and me as the other. I'd pitch, a kid
would hit the ball and run the bases, while Peggy fielded. She'd
race to get the ball and bring it to me. I'd run to tag the kid for

an out. The ball got increasingly slippery with dog slobbers, but surprisingly, the scores turned out to be fairly even.

Depending on what Roy was doing, he could sometimes take Fred with him. Then I'd have some kid-free time to do some writing or work on getting wood. I loved this time among the trees and savored the beauty, freshness, almost divinity of the woods; the hushed, chapel-like feeling of peace. No chainsaws or motors to break the stillness of trees or the breath of wind, the twitter of birds, or the background song of the river. No fumes to mask the delicious scent of cottonwood or pine or pungent earth. When the river froze over, the hush only deepened. Perhaps part of the joy was feeling my own energy, my body active and moving in ways for which it was designed, rather than sitting for hours in a cramped office exercising only my fingers.

Peggy pursued her own explorations, then rushed back to give me a lick on the chin and assess my progress in felling a tree. Sometimes I'd cut two or three dead trunks out of a tangle. Other times I'd concentrate on a large one that I had to saw into several logs before I could manage to drag the pieces home.

Once Peggy spotted a dead tree small enough to tackle on her own. It stood about seven feet, maybe two inches thick at the base. She reached up as high as she could on hind legs and tugged until it came loose at the root. It took a couple of tries to get the balance right, then she proudly carried the little trunk home by herself.

Did I always relish heading out with ax and saw to face the elements? Of course not. Especially not in a cold wind, or when the snow piled deep and crusted and proved hard to walk through. But the enticements of keeping warm and eating hot food proved a mighty motivation. And the enthusiasm of my canine companion mocked my reluctance to get going. She was right, of course. Once I was well into the chore, my gloomy mood shifted almost into exultation, and I thanked God for this opportunity to touch earth and sky and the majesty of trees.

One spring, an old high school friend visited from New York where she lived in an upscale apartment on Fifth Avenue and held a high position in the world of finance. She told me her job was "terribly vital," and I suppose it was. In any case, I think she terribly needed to believe that. But it sounded to my ear that she felt something was missing, that a tiny corner of her soul yearned for that primeval tie to the earth, the satisfaction of a deeper connection. I thought she'd rebel at having to use a privy, but she reminded me how she went to camp for all those summers as a kid, eventually becoming a counselor and teacher. As it turned out, she was more familiar with primitive amenities than I.

We gave her the kids' bedroom, and the dispossessed kids laid out their sleeping bags where they wanted in the living room. She admired the two stoves and exclaimed at the delicious taste of the clear cold water emitted by the pump. (I didn't tell her about its inauspicious beginnings.)

She played softball with the kids in the clearing north of the cabin and especially liked skipping flat stones with them on the river, a talent she drew from her camping years.

Perhaps she wondered how she'd allowed herself to drift so far from that connection with nature she'd loved long ago. According to Thoreau, "In wildness is the preservation of the world," and I would add, "and of mankind."

When Peggy and I dragged home our harvest, tree by tree, I'd sometimes saw it up into stove-length chunks myself, rather than leave it for Roy or the boys. And sometimes I'd split the chunks, learning to wield the ax fairly accurately. Emma, the school cook, stopped by one crisp January day when I was chopping. I told her that I enjoyed it.

"I always did, too, Gay," she said with conviction and just a touch of wistfulness. "When we used wood, I always asked Chuck to leave the chopping for me."

Chores for the kids involved taking the garbage to the trash barrel, burning it (older kids), taking out the ashes from the stoves, household duties, shoveling snow, the normal run-of-the-mill tasks. The major chore for all of us was filling the woodboxes, the one by the large "acorn"-topped heater in the living room, and the box that sat next to the kitchen stove. No wood, no fire, therefore no heat, no cooking and no supper. The progression and consequences were obvious. Not that the kids didn't need encouragement from time to time. If there wasn't enough wood, Sam or Frank would have to chop or saw until there was, and Jenny and Fred could start hauling.

Wielding adult-size saws, axes, and hatchets was dangerous, of course, and Roy bored the kids nearly to tears with
lectures on safety habits.

"Stay clear!" "Give the chopper plenty of room!" "Take
your time!" "BE CAREFUL!"

We kept a box of Band-aids handy, along with alcohol
and iodine. While there were plenty of scrapes, bumps, and
minor cuts, we never had a major accident, for which I was
prayerfully grateful.

The wood chores, more than anything else, forced all of
us to do what we often didn't *want* to do. We might grumble
and resist, we might spout tears, but consequences ruled—
not artificial, parent-induced consequences, but the real thing
born of experience. And we all learned to put this experience
into the framework of a family working together. If one didn't
do his part, someone else had to. If I had big plans for taking
the kids to the library next day, I'd need to make sure we had
enough wood for both days. When the kids came home from
school, they had to pass the woodpile to get to the house.
Was there enough wood available to saw or chop? In the
house they checked the woodboxes. Full or empty? Sometimes
the kids didn't even *need* my reminder to get busy. Once or
twice, the inquiry, "Hey, Ma, when's supper?" was answered
with "No idea. There's no wood to cook it." This didn't happen often.

In later years, Fred said that even though the wood chores
seemed miserable at the time, he knew they were necessary.

He understood that he was making an important contribution to the family. But chores aside, the woods themselves were glorious, and he disappeared into them whenever he could. When the kids were grown, every one of them, including Jenny, spent some time logging professionally, and they all loved working in the forest.

Fred never minded playing alone. He sometimes set up elaborate scenarios with toy soldiers; or farm scenes with tiny horses, cows, and tractors; or construction sites with larger Tonka trucks. We always kept plenty of paper and crayons for kids to draw with. He liked this, and soon began drawing maps and house plans, which became detailed landscapes and castles. When asked what he wanted to be when he grew up, he answered, "half artist, half cowboy, and half everything else."

The kitten Willy had grown into quite a character. While sometimes a welcome playmate, he could also drive the kids crazy. He had a personality similar to his mother Toots's without her irascibility. Fred liked to build complex Lincoln Log constructions, and Willy would crawl inside, then leap around with great joy, scattering logs in all directions. Sometimes he wandered over to the guitar standing in the corner and amused himself by plucking the strings. His favorite place to sleep was under the covers in Jenny's bed, day or night. He was harder to give away than most of the kittens, but we found him a good family. For quite a while Willy "wrote" to us, reporting on his exploits and signing his missives with a green pawprint. He sat on their bookcase and ate the ivy leaves, or he'd run up and down the piano keys, furthering his enjoyment of music, or take a running leap onto their table and slide all the way across on the tablecloth. They were quite taken with him, and Fred could make his constructions in peace.

Fred was pleased to have one popular toy all to himself—a "phono-viewer." Constructed of red plastic and shaped somewhat like a small TV set, it had a screen, a turntable on top, and a place for filmstrips. He set the filmstrip in the slot, started the record, then listened to the story unfold while watching the slides appear on the screen. This was a gift from Gammy and Grampa, who kept the story-sets coming for Christmases and birthdays for several years. These included fairy tales, abbreviated literary classics such as *Robinson Crusoe*, "Paul Revere's Ride," and *Swiss Family Robinson,* as well as historical reenactments: the fight at the Alamo, the Battle of Bunker Hill with "Don't shoot until you see the whites of their eyes," and the like. The grand favorite was Custer's Last Stand, delivered poetically in a cultured accent of indeterminate origin ("Geowge A. Custah"), with stirring sounds of trumpets, war whoops, and galloping hoofbeats. Most of the stories have been mercifully forgotten over time, but Fred played "Custah's" Last Stand so often, parts of it are engraved on my memory. "He was young for a general but he'd earned his rank, fighting battle after battle on the side of the Yank … And he fought against the

Pawnee, the Cheyenne, and the Sioux, and he WON!" Ta-da-dahhh!! Drumrolls. Hoofbeats.

Even though the verses went on to mourn the sad demise of the general, the kids cheered the Indians.

We had scads of books: an ever-changing stack of library books, as well as our own, which included comics such as Donald Duck, Bugs Bunny, Classic Comics, Superman. Fred spent a lot of time with all the books, perhaps looking at pictures, perhaps reading from memory all the well-loved ones, probably reading some on his own, even though he hadn't yet officially learned to read. Jenny had loved playing school with Fred and their friend Lois, when we lived next door to her. Now that Jenny was in school herself, she'd take her little brother to the tree house on afternoons or weekends and work on teaching him to read.

Sam enjoyed boys' animal adventure stories. He started with Rutherford Montgomery and Jim Kjelgaard (including *Big Red*) and soon made it to Jack London. Sam sometimes wrote his favorite authors and even got answers. I found the first draft of one of his letters stuffed into my diary:

Dear Mr. [William O.] Steele,

I am 11 years old.

I like your books. In fact I think you are the best author in the whole world. I have read all your books I know of, but three, and have enjoyed them all to the utmost. Ever since I learned to read I have liked books like yours, but could never find very many. But when I found Flaming Arrows, Wilderness Journey, Buffalo Knife, *and several others I thought I had reached book paradise. Please keep writing books.*

Sincerely, Sam Collier

The kids were all readers, which seemed perfectly natural to Roy and me. Before long, they were enjoying the Hardy Boys, *Rascal, Tom Sawyer, Huck Finn, Treasure Island,* the books by Lloyd Alexander, and later, thanks to Reader's Digest Condensed Books, *The Hunchback of Notre Dame* and *The Big Sky.* We got "kiddie" dictionaries early on, Roy had his favorite dictionary from the forties (with the "right" pronunciations), and I kept an unabridged dictionary, as up-to-date as we could afford. We were always looking up words.

We set up a vocabulary clothesline, partly in response to the "Mommy, what does this mean?" questions. We strung a three-foot length of cord along the wall above the kitchen woodbox, then cut three-by-five index cards in half and paper-clipped them onto the cord. I printed our new word on one side along with the definition; on the other side, the word stood alone. After the kids knew what the word meant and could use it in a sentence, the card was turned over. We could sneak a peek at the definition if needed, but generally it didn't take long before all of us could use the word comfortably. We even started adding words from *Reader's Digest's* "It Pays to Increase your Word Power." I never realized the kids' vocabulary could make a problem at school.

Frank, especially, loved using big words, starting a lifelong habit. One thing led to another, and after a while, he was reading my books, even Dostoyevsky and Tolstoy, interspersed with bug identification books and Carl Barks' famous, often history-based, Uncle Scrooge comics—an eclectic diet.

The kids' reading habits, as well as their use of big words, seemed to nonplus the newer teachers. Perhaps they thought the kids were swearing, which, depending on what they'd been reading lately, might have been the case. Sam and Jenny did pretty well in class, but Frank struggled with school, possibly because what he wanted to do at any given moment rarely jibed with what the teacher wanted him to do. Staying in his seat was a concept that didn't make much sense to him, unless he had a good book to read, which in third or fourth grade usually meant conventional early-readers rather than comics or thousand-page novels. One exasperated young teacher tied him into his seat with her pantyhose. However, since she didn't think to remove the scissors from his desk, he was soon wandering again, while her pantyhose lay in pieces on the floor. I think Sam or Jenny reported that with glee; I didn't hear about it from the teacher.

One thing we *did* hear about was the time Frank was supposed to give a report on current news. With no TV and no funds at the time for subscribing to a weekly news magazine, we used what was available: *Labor*, the union paper that came to Roy after he started working for a trucking outfit and had to join the Teamsters. Unfortunately, in mim-

icking some political figure of the time, Roy always pro-
nounced the word ponderously as *Lay-bohr.* Frank reproduced
the pronunciation in class when he introduced his report
"from my father's *Lay-bohr* magazine." It seems the teacher
was unfamiliar with this legitimate, if narrowly focused and
possibly biased, news source. To her ear it sounded like "my
father's *Playboy* magazine," and she went ballistic, stopping
the report before it began.

Then there was the time I got a tentative call from one
of the mothers who, after initial greetings and comments on
the weather, got to the point of the call.

"Are you really moving to Borneo?"

"What?"

"Well, my neighbor told me her daughter said you were
moving to Borneo. The kids are all talking about it."

I had to ponder that for a moment but eventually figured
out how the rumor originated. Several days earlier, on one of
our wilder mornings (it being a bad-hair day with thoughts
of circus posters from my childhood coming to mind), I had
announced in exasperation, "I feel like the Wild Woman
from Borneo!" The mother and I chuckled together over the
progression of rumor, but I wondered what other stories
might be making the rounds.

Apparently problems were stacking up. We had come to
the attention of the Social Services people who were concerned
about this benighted family living in the woods without
plumbing and, far worse in this modern age of 1967, without

television! How would the children keep up in the world? What sort of dreadful things were they learning, or *not* learning, at home? What about their strange vocabulary? What about the onerous chores (such as cutting wood) they were forced to do? What about the wild woman who would be returning to Borneo, dragging her children along with her, just as soon as she could make a break for it? And truly horrifying, what about the fate of a young child at home during the day, probably dressed in dirt-covered hand-me-downs (not too far off, there), with a wild woman for a mother and a father who "rolled his own" and was addicted to lewd magazines?

I wasn't aware of any of this until we had an unannounced visitor. I'd been having one of my normal hectic mornings. The house was a mess, my hair a tangle, my clothes the grubbies I usually wore. I sometimes fantasized about keeping a neat, spotless house—how lovely it would be to always be ready for company!—but it seemed beyond me. Maybe the kids should have helped more with this, but somehow the wood chores superseded everything else. They had to come first, and school was next. Roy and I both encouraged getting homework done and putting effort into reports and projects. Writing grandparents, working at 4-H projects and record books, and similar activities filled any leftover crannies of time.

On this day Fred had disappeared outside, and I was stirring fruit cocktail into the red Jell-O I was fixing for supper, when the dog set up a furious pazoo at the gate. Just what I needed: company. Maybe Peggy would scare them

ARE YOU REALLY MOVING TO BORNEO?

off. She had accomplished that once when two unsavory-looking men turned up in the yard, seemingly to no good purpose. I'd hung on to her collar and did nothing to discourage her ferocious snarls until they left.

Now I looked out to see an intrepid lady in a dress (not a neighbor, then) braving the dog and coming through the gate. A barking German shepherd can be intimidating, but the woman continued walking, with determination, to the house. Rats! I took a quick look around, saw that trying to tidy things up was hopeless, and set the pan of Jell-O on the edge of the table where there was a little space. I heard the crash behind me just as I made it to the porch door. Apparently there wasn't quite enough space.

I opened the door, yelled at Peggy, smiled (I think) at the woman, and failed to stop Toots from dashing in with something in her mouth. Not a kitten. I think it was a mouse. The lady wasn't selling magazines or Avon and seemed to think she should come in despite my lack of enthusiasm for the idea. She introduced herself in the doorway as a social worker and—wham! In the space of one second, I saw the entire house in its current condition and my own fetching appearance. These combined with pictures in my mind of social workers I'd read about in the past "rescuing" screaming children from neglectful parents and hauling them off to orphanages and foster homes, while bereft mothers wailed and fathers struggled with local law enforcement. Actually, thinking about it now, I suspect the visit was due to a unilateral

163

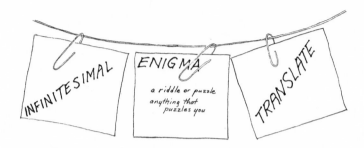

INFINITESIMAL

ENIGMA
a riddle or puzzle
anything that
puzzles you

TRANSLATE

report from a new teacher. The older, long-time teacher already knew Sam and knew the rest of the family, as well, from various school functions. She may have thought us a bit odd, but not dangerous, nor would she have been shocked by life without TV or plumbing.

I led the lady into the kitchen. Herbert sat by the partly congealed red mess on the floor, licking his paw. As the lady stepped into the room, he stabbed a grape with a right claw, looked up with a thoughtful expression, and conveyed the grape to his mouth. "That's Herbert," I said by way of introduction, not knowing what else to say. I fumbled through some stupid excuses for the mess and hoped that Toots would stay wherever she was hiding.

The lady looked around, keeping a remarkably blank expression, noted the humming refrigerator, and said something about electricity. "Oh yes, of course we have electricity!" I beamed. She took in the pitcher pump at the sink and asked about plumbing. I avoided the question by pointing out the vocabulary clothesline.

She marched into the living room and glanced into the war zone that I usually thought of as the kids' bedroom. I rushed around her to clear a spot on the sofa, piling books on the floor. She sat. I cleared off a chair for myself. We conversed. I couldn't think of anything I had to offer her (Roy had finished off the Oreos for breakfast, and it was too late for the Jell-O). She noted that there was no TV, even though we had electricity. I noted that we had a lot of books and the kids loved to read. We talked about the three kids in school. I thought she seemed disappointed that they were doing fairly well, despite some idiosyncrasies, but perhaps that was just my perception. By now, my heart was pounding. I felt I was fighting a real battle to keep our kids. I wondered whether there were legal papers involved in purloining children or if Social Services could take them unannounced, direct from school. Finally, she asked if there wasn't another child.

"Yes," I said. "Fred will be starting school next fall."

"I'd like to meet him," she said. Probably wanted to see if he knew his name, was wearing clothes, and could speak at least a rudimental English.

"I'll call him." I found him out back, deeply involved in arranging soldiers, horses, Indians, sticks, and stones in various patterns across carefully constructed dirt piles. "Please come in," I said. "A lady wants to meet you." It took a couple of tries to get through to him.

Back inside, I smiled brightly while waiting for Fred to appear. He finally did, and, dripping good, honest, sandy Wyoming soil, stood in the doorway.

"Hello, little boy," the lady said with an ingratiating smile. "And what is your name?"

He stood a minute, looked her up and down, then strode forward with straight face, dirty hand outstretched. "Howdy, Ma'am," he said, his five-year-old voice replicating the tone and accent of the phono-viewer record. "The name's Custah. General Geowge A. Custah."

She was a professional, all right. Though apparently stunned into silence, she shook his grimy hand, rolled her eyes once toward me, then rose to go, as the general turned and marched back to his unfinished business. For three months afterward, I was afraid to answer the phone and cringed when Peggy announced someone coming. But I never heard from her again, and no one turned up to impound the children.

MA, A BUTTON CAME OFF

WE'D LIVED IN THE CABIN A YEAR when Fred started school in the fall of 1967. By late August, harlequin splotches of yellow and gold claimed a branch here, a bush there, and soon the color splashed over the trees. The school bus bounced along the back roads, gathering children with funereal faces. Chuck drove up to the gate and waved. The kids (all ready and waiting that first day—three cheers for Mother) were sucked in, and in a flash of gaiety, the blotch of yellow winked through the trees and disappeared.

The quiet that remained matched the emptiness in the pit of my stomach. For the first time in many years, no little ones rustled and banged, asked interminable questions, or disappeared, leaving a resounding silence that made me wonder what sort of trouble they were getting into. It should have been glorious. The hours were mine to order as I wished. Uninterrupted, I'd have time to think, to concentrate, to *write!* I would rejoice, do you hear?

I turned to the dog. She sat with me on the front step, gazing into the distance, presumably following the bus with her ears. "Got that?" I said. "We are now enjoying Peace and Quiet."

She cocked an eyebrow at me and stepped off into the bed of woodbine where she made herself comfortable and, whether by instinct or design, proceeded to look noble and worthy.

"I will treat myself to another cup of coffee," I said loudly and went into the cabin. The pitcher pump at the sink hissed at me as I walked past, and burped a couple of times down deep inside. It had never settled down to quiet obedience, although its water now ran clear and pure.

The pump's complaints would have echoed emptily in the kitchen, but the fire still crackled in the stove, and the kettle steamed with an agreeable purr. Almost enough water for a full cup of instant. Clearing a place on the table with my elbow, I set the cup down and pulled on my chair. It didn't budge.

"Sorry," I said to Herbert without even bothering to look down. The cat weighed a ton and would never move without forcible ejection. He'd been known to crash to the floor if pushed off his perch without a gentle, ceremonious awakening. Although often in the way, Herbert was a good companion, quiet and rock-steady. Not wanting to disturb his reverie on the kitchen chair, I sat on the edge of the woodbox. Most of the other chairs were piled with stuff anyway.

The warmth of the stove felt good. The briskness of the morning hinted at frost to come. I didn't want to think about it. The coffee tasted pretty dull, not the least celebrationist. A festive mood escaped me. Perhaps I needed to toss around some confetti. I examined the room critically. On second thought, I didn't need confetti—I already had it.

But of course, this kind of self-indulgence couldn't last long—too much to do. I revved up the fire to heat the bucket of water preparatory to washing dishes and getting on with my other chores. But first, a quick trip to the river wouldn't hurt at all. Peggy caught my intent the moment I stepped out the door. She raced ahead of me down the path.

With each gust of wind, leaves cascaded from the cottonwoods hanging over the stream. The leaves bobbed and floated on the water, clustered in eddies, and formed golden mosaics that glinted and shifted gently on the surface. Peggy plunged into the water, rearranging the existing leaf patterns into paisley swirls. I sat on the bank, threw sticks for her to chase and snatch from the river, and laughed with her until she climbed out and shook violently. Now she was dry and I was wet. I watched the leaves, wishing I could hold on to their beauty, keep them gleaming on their branches like stained-glass windowlets against the brilliant blue, keep them from sliding away down the current of life. What was it Connie had said one day recently in our kitchen? "You'll remember this time as the best years of your life." Was he right?

Sometimes I thought he was. For now, I was grateful to be right here. I loved the land, loved the river, loved the sparkle and shadow, the animals, life itself. The kids seemed to be developing into good, decent people, and, as far as I could tell, they loved this land as much as Roy and I did.

Peggy tossed her head with a guttural *growf.*

"Right," I said. "Back to work."

In the cabin, I refilled the teakettle and set it to boil while I washed the dishes, then poured the boiling rinse water over them and left them to dry. The quiet seemed friendlier since we'd had our time by the river. Ahh, now to sit down and finish the humorous story I'd agreed to do for a local dog-training newsletter. And then maybe I'd even have time to spend on my novel or another chapter of the horse book.

Or walk over to see Ellie. I spent as much time as possible helping her with the horses and dogs, all while soaking up valuable experience. Sometimes I babysat the animals while she was away at fairs and shows throughout the region. The kids helped too, when they were home, and in exchange, she gave them all riding lessons. Jenny, especially, took to horses and wanted to spend all her time with them.

We spent considerable time taking photos with book il-lustrations in mind. Some of these photo sessions included the boys, but Jenny was the one who had the patience to stick it out while we took picture after picture to illustrate exactly the point we were trying to make. Getting it "right" wasn't easy. Did the horse look alert, ears forward, feet set squarely? Was the rider's chin up, hands and legs placed just right, posture good, position in the saddle correct, and so on? We had to wait until the prints were returned (no instant digital previews in those days) to see if they were usable.

Sam began helping Ellie with chores before school and on weekends, mucking out stalls or grooming horses before classes. I enjoyed seeing a youngster gain confidence in handling horses: haltering, tying a quick-release knot, working with currycomb and brush, picking up each foot to clean the hoof. I knew how fortunate we were that the kids could learn from an expert how to work safely with 800- to 1000-pound animals, to perform each task the proper way, and the reasons why.

I was learning, too. I'd taken riding lessons all during my high school years, but that had been once a week at a riding academy miles from home. On occasion, Ellie gave me lessons in the corral or outdoor arena. As my confidence and ability grew, she sometimes had me ride a green horse in the corral while she controlled him from a long line (called longeing). Other days we rode out together through the pastures or up onto the lower slopes of Jelm Mountain. This trail experience was part of the training she gave to young horses or a way for her to exercise her stallion. I gloried in these rides. They combined the beauty, sounds, and smells of the rangeland with the exhilarating appreciation of horseflesh—the power, the movement, the feeling of unity with another of God's creatures.

By June of 1968, Ellie and I felt we'd revised enough on the book to send it back to Steinkraus at Van Nostrand. His letter, almost by return mail, threw us into a frenzy of writing and rewriting: "Both the substance and the arrangement of the new outline strike me as excellent, and I would be delighted to have an opportunity to see the finished manuscript before you submit it elsewhere." No big rush, however, as he was preparing his team for the 1968 Olympics to be held in Mexico City (where, incidentally, he was to win a gold medal in Individual Jumping).

At the end of September, with our revisions in hand, Steinkraus gave us a firm acceptance for Van Nostrand, asking for the remaining text and illustrations within the next month. Giddy with delight, we worked feverishly, sure now of publication of our skillfully coached masterpiece, though we hadn't yet signed a contract. We sent the rest, and sighing with relief, settled back to wait for fame and fortune.

What can I say, other than "Oops!" The publisher sold out to another company, which abandoned Van Nostrand's trade list along with its editor. Steinkraus was left holding several firmly accepted but as yet uncontracted manuscripts. "Surprised and disappointed," he offered to serve as our agent at no fee.

But all's well that ends sometime. He took the manuscript back to Doubleday and Ellin Roberts, and this time it was accepted. Ellin was an old-time editor who believed her job was to work with and for the author, saying that the publishers had enough going for them. In February, she sent us a six-page, single-spaced, margin-to-margin letter of suggestions, corrections, and comments. She knew the horse business as well as the editing business, and with this invaluable guideline, we went back to work. Two years later, after much back and forth with Ellin, dropping one chapter, combining several others, and adding two more, along with more photos and drawings, we delivered the final manuscript in December 1972. *Basic Horsemanship: English and Western* came out in the spring of '74, ten years after Ellie and I had started on it.

All the work and expert help paid off. The book stayed in print for over thirty years, and we added two others to the series. Experience paid off, too, because each additional book took only five years to complete.

✳ ⸰ ✳ ⸰ ✳ ⸰ ✳

Another avenue of moneymaking potential turned out to be my guitar. From as early as I could remember, my grandfather strummed his old guitar and sang to me as he'd done to my mother:

> *A little mouse once had a house*
> *'Twas made of leaves and grass.*
> *She went away one summer day,*
> *The time did gaily pass.*
> > *Mousie, mousie, you should watch your children,*
> > *Mousie, mousie, you should stay at home.*

He taught me to play, and the guitar became for me a crutch that helped me emerge from the debilitating shyness of childhood. An audience struck me dumb. School plays were agony. The elementary teachers soon learned to cast me in non-speaking roles, preferably disguised as a water-sprite or wind-fairy, dressed in swirls of home-dyed, blue-green cheesecloth, swaying silently in the background. But with a guitar as a buffer between me and all those eyes, something to hold onto and occupy my fingers, I gradually climbed my way out of the shyness swamp. Most of the way. Most of the time.

I loved old folksongs, eventually learning hundreds of them. And so I began teaching folk guitar to kids who were old enough, first Sam, then Jenny and other kids in the neighborhood (Frank's taste ran more to classical recordings than do-it-yourself folk). This sometimes earned money, but more often fresh produce or mending. This was especially appreciated because, although my mother had made many of my clothes until I was a teenager, I never learned to sew. Even when the kids were little, they'd say, "Ma, a button came off, but never mind, I'll fix it myself." Somehow in my hands, needle and thread took on lives of their own, deliberately tangling up, producing Gordian knots, pricking my fingers, and leaving bloody tracks on the fabric.

When Ellie started her summer horsemanship school, girls attended from all over the country, and several signed up for guitar lessons (paid in advance). Our cabin was only a few hundred yards from Ellie's big house, so this was convenient. Either my kids could come with me or manage home alone, or the girls could walk up to the cabin for lessons.

By this time, I was feeling the need for more expertise in my playing, and with some money I'd saved from summer earnings, I decided to take a Community Education class in Intermediate Guitar, sponsored by the university. Ellie was with me when I went to sign up.

"Oh, I'm so sorry," the registration lady said. "I'm afraid that class is cancelled. The man who was going to teach it moved away."

Disappointed, I said, "Well, how about the beginner class?" I figured I'd probably learn something new in any case.

"Same teacher."

At this point, Ellie jumped in. "You could teach it yourself!" She turned to the lady and began extolling my virtuosities, while I sputtered away in vain. By the time those two had finished, I was signed up as teacher, paid by the university, of both beginning and intermediate guitar.

Finally cramming my word in edgewise, I insisted, "*Folk* guitar!" I didn't want any prospective student imagining that Segovia Jr. had arrived on the scene—or Chet Atkins Jr. either. In a moment of further inspiration, wondering how on earth I was going to fill up two hours with the little I knew, I suggested combining the hands-on lessons with mini-lectures on history of the guitar and the development of folk music. The deal was sealed.

My head reeling, I realized I had about two weeks before confronting my first classes. These became a very intense two weeks. Thanks to my collection of books (by now I was reviewing folksong books for *Library Journal*, along with horse books), I had most of the information available. The public and university libraries filled in the gaps. I had only to plan the history lessons, write them up, write down and notate the songs with melody and chords (some of this I'd already done for the children I'd worked with), get everything copied for handouts, and set up a syllabus of sorts for the Community Ed people to have on file. I began getting phone calls from prospective students: "I know three chords. Should I sign up for Beginning or Intermediate?"

The lessons helped out a little financially, but after another year had passed, it was apparent we needed more funds to get through daily living. I eventually applied for Real Work at the university. Roy wasn't happy about this, and his do-it-the-old-way principles came into play. I could work my tail off at home, which either he didn't appreciate or didn't notice, by which I mean that although he'd thank me for doing various chores, he didn't really understand the amount of effort it took. I think he thought it all came naturally, and therefore easily, to me. I remembered some rural families I knew, both in Vermont and in Wyoming, where roles were basically defined as man-in-the-fields and woman-in-the-house. But when the man needed help to get his work done, he didn't hesitate to call out his wife. In the evening, he'd sit in his easy chair to wait for supper and complain that it wasn't ready on time. But would he help in the kitchen? No way—that was woman's work.

That wasn't the case with Roy. He did help at home when he could. He even changed diapers when the kids were little. This help didn't extend to cooking, however. He'd either wait without complaining or kindly suggest his usual solution: "We can just eat Oreos and milk." But for me to actually apply for a job? That went against the grain of old-time tradition.

I'd go along with Roy on a lot of things (such as living without plumbing), and I'd listen to his reasonings or rantings, depending on the situation. But when I believed it was crucial, I'd usually storm ahead with what *I* thought was the right thing to do. And he generally resigned himself without further battles. Not that I was always right, of course, but this time I thought I was.

I landed a temporary, part-time position in the university's agricultural information office, a job that relieved our financial distress a bit without earning enough to threaten Roy's position as chief breadwinner of the household. I loved this working with words, layouts, and other intricacies of publication. Best of all, the job furthered my editorial skills and paved the way for future possibilities in writing.

Roy accepted this for the most part, especially since I could schedule my work time to be relatively unobtrusive as far as he was concerned. We'd already been dovetailing our work, meetings, and evening guitar classes so that one or the other of us would be home with the kids. When a friend of ours from Vermont came out to visit us after his wife died, he met Ellie, a fellow New Englander. Eventually they married, and Bill and his children—Carleton and Lynn, both older than our kids, and George, who was Frank's age—moved into the big house with Ellie. Sometimes Carleton or Lynn would watch our kids if both Roy and I had to be away.

Ellie had been renting the big house and outbuildings from the owner downriver, and now she and Bill began looking for a place of their own just as we were. Bill had been a dairy farmer in Vermont, and he wanted to raise beef cattle, for which he needed pasture and hayland. Ellie needed the security of her own place to develop her horsemanship school and growing reputation as a breeder of fine Arabians. Perhaps if they found their ranch, we'd be able to move into the big house, the ideal castle that had loomed ahead as we first drove down the highway all those years ago.

And then, a new and surprising wrinkle turned up in my life. I received a letter from the county commissioners, saying I'd been appointed to the Board of Directors of our county public library. How could this have happened? Was I chosen because we used the library so much, taking books home by the boxful? Maybe someone had made a mistake. How would I fit in with the other four board members—all people of substance and stature in the community, including a lawyer, a banker, a college professor? My first meeting would be next evening.

What on earth would I wear? As a rule, I dressed in Levi's, tennis shoes, and Roy's old shirts while I worked around the house or foraged for firewood. Fancy dress for school and 4-H meetings amounted to freshly clean work clothes. Rummaging beneath piles of old boots and junk on the closet floor, I unearthed a pair of high heels from my pre-marriage days. I could wear them several whole hours at a time if I didn't have to stand too much. And crammed back in the corner I found my one dress. Actually, I kind of liked it, a tailored rose cotton shirtwaist with long sleeves and a full skirt. It fit well, looked pretty good, and would drip-dry without ironing. It would have to do.

But it needed washing. Normally, we bundled our clothes off to the Laundromat in town. But today Roy had the pickup. A trip to town wasn't possible. There was nothing for it but to wash the dress in the river. I grabbed a plastic bottle of dish soap, called the dog, and carried the dress down the path, past the privy, and along the riverbank.

The alders and shrub willows always smelled sweet, but now, sun-warmed and accented with the baskety smell of drying grass, the scent seemed even lovelier than usual. I stopped, closed my eyes, and breathed it in. Further on, at my favorite spot, the bank eased into the stream. Water slapped against the rocks. Sunlight filtered through tall cottonwoods on the south bank, dappling the leaf-strewn ripples with shade and sparkle. A soft breeze, instead of the earlier gusts, rode the river eastward.

I piled shoes and socks in the grass, rolled up my pants, waded out onto the rounded, water-worn stones, then paused to look upstream. The river promised so much. We never knew what might come around the bend, float into our lives, slide on past, and disappear beyond the next bend—logs, leafy branches, mallards and Canada geese, a beachball, beavers, otters, a red shirt, kayakers. Now, millions of gold leaves flashed like spilled sequins on the ripples.

I stepped into deeper water, crouched down to soak the dress, watched the rose turn deep maroon. Peggy gave up trying to get me to throw sticks for her to chase and pursued her own investigations. I rubbed a few drops of soap into the soiled spots and tossed the bottle back onto the bank, then settled to serious washing, my feet cold in the water, my back hot in the sun. I became absorbed in this mundane task, became conscious of myself washing my dress in the river, a member of a timeless sisterhood, women of the Ganges, the Niger, the Huang Ho. Perhaps a pioneer woman had washed her dress here, her feet slipping on these same rocks.

Magpies squawked overhead, and I laughed out loud at this absurdity. Here was a library trustee, a member of a Board of Directors, washing her only dress in a river—surely the only trustee in the state of Wyoming to be doing so, the only trustee in the whole United States, maybe even the whole world, to wash her dress in a river, hang it to dry among the cottonwoods, and then wear it, straight-faced, to a board meeting.

There, I would attempt wit and competence, I would pretend dignity and confidence and sophistication. And I would do these things wrapped in the soft, fresh feel and scent of Wyoming river-water and Wyoming wind. I would draw courage from the delicious secret of a cotton dress with the humble provenance of joy and beauty, hilarity and absurdity—and perhaps even a sense of destiny.

Back at the cabin, I found a clothes hanger, then hung the dress on a nearby tree limb where it could sway in the wind. I got on with my other chores, but whether glancing out through a window, or looking up from chopping wood outside, my eyes were drawn to the waving fabric. I saw the dress turn lighter, dancing more and more freely as it dried. And I knew all this was right and good, and just as things should be.

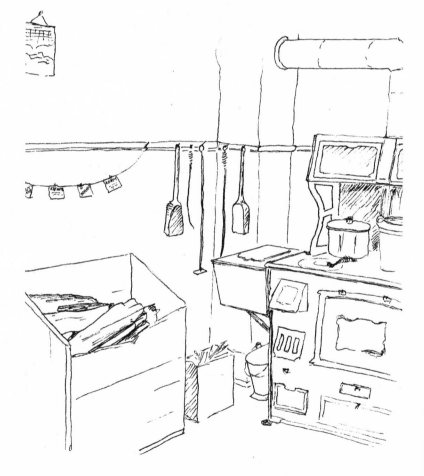

THAT'S THE PROBLEM!
A DIETER!

HAD I EXPECTED, NOW that all the kids were in school, to rearrange my fractured and frazzled lifestyle into clearer focus? Ho ho. Instead, the school commitments mushroomed to fill my imagined extra time. My involvement in programs, Parent-Teacher Social activities, teachers' aide duties, 4-H projects and fairs, and other community doings expanded exponentially.

For one thing, the PTS meetings involved entertainment, which someone had to organize. Once, Emma had called me when a program was cancelled at the last minute. "Can you show the slides from your African safari tomorrow night?"

"What?"

"You know, your safari. The program you gave at Centennial last year."

"That was someone else, Emma. We've never even been out of the country." Maybe she'd gotten it confused with the Borneo rumor.

"Really? Are you sure? Well, we need a program. Can you do something?"

"I guess we could show some slides from Vermont." Well, almost as exotic as the veldt.

I spent the rest of the morning sorting our slides, gathering shots of the fluffy-white apple orchard in May, the velvety green hills of summer, the fiery fall maple trees, snowdrifts and snow tunnels, and the maple sugaring process of early spring.

While showing the slides at the meeting, I told about the first settlers back in the early 1700s. A man looking for a place of his own would walk up the Connecticut River valley carrying rifle and ax, a single cutting of lilac, and a bar of soap. He would have been instructed by his wife that, if he found a likely spot to settle, he should first try to lather the soap in the stream. If it lathered easily, the water would be soft and the site suitable. If not, he should keep looking. Hard water made life even more difficult than it already was. The lilac cutting would be planted when the right site was found, a marker for the future. I showed pictures of stone walls and huge lilac bushes with their nearby row of rhubarb. Even if the foundations had disappeared, the rhubarb and lilac marked where the first house had been.

The slide show proved a success, with considerable raving about the beautiful photos, the beautiful countryside, and what brilliant photographers we were. Of course, I'd learned from Pappy, my artist grandfather. Good composition, careful focus and adjustment of shutter speed and f-stops, and all that—but the big secret of a good show seemed a bit simplistic to me, though apparently novel to the audience. You picked out only your best shots. You didn't include the fuzzy ones, the over- or under-exposed, the shots where half the frame was covered by your thumb, the portraits with the top of the head cut off. But I'd never been as exacting as Pappy. He saved only perfect pictures, even if it meant throwing away three-quarters or more of the roll.

The kids were getting old enough to begin evaluating their teachers. Fred wrote a letter to his grandma: "Dear Gammy. This year we have a new teacher. She is a nice teacher and she is my favorite one so far. Her one problem is she is sort of strict, but that isn't too bad."

At supper one night, Sam reported on the upper grades teacher. "Boy, our new one sure is crabby."

"And she never smiles," Jenny added. I noticed in the school photos taken that year, she indeed appeared grim and beset.

"Does she eat with you?" Roy inquired. This seemed a given, considering that the school was located miles from restaurants or even a deli. And besides, with Emma for a cook, who would want to eat anywhere else? The teachers always joined their kids at the lunch tables.

"Well, she sits with us," Sam said. "But she doesn't eat anything except a can of no-fat-something."

Roy slammed his hand on the table. "Lyndon! That's the problem then. A dieter! Dieters are always crabby; they should never teach kids. That should always be the first rule when hiring a teacher: find out if she eats." He grumbled along in the same vein while I considered that bringing a can of diet-food to the table was certainly no way to win brownie points with Emma.

But then, our family wasn't winning many brownie points with the teachers either. Occasionally we even garnered shocked reprimands. In an effort to enforce the manners supposedly taught at home, teachers had the kids wait for grace before plunging into their noon meal. One child was selected each day to do the honors. This generally followed the "God-is-great-God-is-good-and-we-thank-Him-for-this-food-amen" model. Quick and familiar (although the older boys sometimes tried to slip in, "Good bread, good meat, good God, let's eat").

Fred branched out on his own. Having accompanied me for a couple of years when I was giving guitar lessons and studying cowboy songs and lore for my History of Folk Music lectures, he'd been exposed to colorful chuck-wagon language. When it was his turn to say grace, he burst out confidently:

> *Up to my lips and over my gums—*
> *Look out, guts! Here she comes!*

Jenny reported this in some shock, but the older boys thought it was hilarious.

As our kids each reached the magical age of ten, they were allowed to join the 4-H Club, a vital part of rural community life. We didn't yet have our own livestock, but Sam started out with leathercraft, using borrowed tools. After a while he acquired his own tools and was soon crafting belts, wallets, and purses. Frank jumped right into entomology. Now instead of simply finding bugs, we were actively hunting various species. He learned the correct procedure for killing and mounting insects. To my immeasurable relief, he no longer stored them in his pockets. Our school-bus-driver-jack-of-all-trades neighbor, Chuck, made him a glass-topped box in which the bugs could be displayed with others of their species, each neatly and scientifically labeled. Roy and I joked that helping Frank with identification was driving us buggy.

With all the 4-H meetings to go to, along with the school functions, there developed a steady flow of kids back and forth among neighbors for project meetings, as different parents accepted leadership for the various projects. Considering the distance between the far-flung ranches, transportation involved logistics of some magnitude. Kids rode home with each other on the school bus, caught a ride with another family who was going to the meeting, stayed overnight, and so on. I needed to make notes on which kid was where.

This kind of continual calculation and logistics planning made my head whirl, and I was glad to have the river to run to whenever I could find a few moments.

One sparkly fall day, I stretched out on the grass at my favorite riverside beach for a quick break before heading back up the path to ever-waiting chores. Gusts of wind swayed the cottonwoods and blew golden leaves into the river. A round, orange face appeared at eye-level, and Herbert, apparently having decided I was settled for a few minutes, climbed onto my stomach and hunkered down in comfort. Both he and Toots had been with us a long time in cat years, and both were showing signs of age.

Herbert was such a placid cat, just his presence had a calming effect on me. His absence, in fact, could be cause for concern. I remembered two occasions where his disappearance caused all of us acute anguish.

The first was in Vermont when we were all packed up to leave for Wyoming and he sat waiting for us in the road. The second disappearance occurred later in the trip. It had been after dark when we stopped at a motel and had our usual bustle and confusion settling in. Air conditioning wasn't common in the early '60s, and the weather was warm, the room hot. We opened the windows wide, after checking to make sure they had screens, and finally got the kids to bed. I was about to climb in when Roy casually wondered where Herbert was hiding. We searched everywhere, including the dresser drawers. No Herbert. Then we noticed that one window screen wasn't latched, and we remembered seeing him sitting on the sill earlier, washing his face. If he had even nudged the screen, it would have swung open enough for him to slip out, which certainly had happened. He could have been gone for hours. Only a miracle had prevented Toots from finding escape also.

I dressed and looked out. A wisp of moon cast a dim light in the alley out back. The kids were all asleep, so I crawled out the window. So did Roy. Going out the door would have meant a long trip around the motel, assuming we could even find the right window at the back. He went in one direction, I went in the other, calling "Herbert!" softly into the night. Hard to know how loud to call. I certainly didn't want to wake all the neighborhood dogs and have the police routed out. On the other hand, poor Herbert was out on his own in a strange town with untold dangers. He probably wasn't even aware that *some* dogs don't like cats. I hoped he'd be overjoyed to hear a familiar voice and come running. I tried to sound tempting, as though I were carrying around a bowl of shrimp and chicken tidbits, all for him.

No Herbert. He could have gone miles. I checked back in the room—kids still asleep—met Roy who also had experienced no luck, and went out again. Finally, beginning to feel really creepy at wandering through back alleys forlornly paging Herbert, I spied a shape in an abandoned lot that, yes, that moved! It seemed to be washing its face. I made my way through weeds and cans, trying not to kick anything noisy. He let me pick him up. Was he happy to see me? No, he seemed put out that I'd interrupted his exotic adventures. Back in the motel, he settled for cheese and bologna, cut into bite-size pieces, and daintily conveyed them to his mouth with his right paw.

Smiling at the memory, I enjoyed the *now* of this moment—the companionship of Herbert and Peggy, who lay down beside us, and the burble and beauty of this spot by the river. And now that the kids were all in school, I could spend a little more time here, and also at Connie and Dena's place, the Hansen ranch just a few miles upstream, where I began to expand my own ranch education.

Connie told endless stories of growing up there after he and his folks moved down from their mountain home, of raising cattle and goats, of ghosts and water-rights wars, of hard and good times. One of his ghost stories, as I remember him telling it, involved a helpful apparition.

As a kid, Connie had set out one evening to find the milk cows. They'd apparently wandered far upstream through the long meadows, and he was tired and annoyed at them. As he trudged along, he saw the cows in the distance heading toward him. They were herded by a man in a strange, almost Tyrolean costume with lederhosen and suspenders like an Alpine yodeler. As they got closer, Connie still couldn't recognize the man in the funny hat with the feather. He lifted his arm to wave and call out his thanks, and suddenly the man dissolved. Connie could never explain it, but felt grateful anyway.

On a hot summer day, Connie would sometimes lie on his stomach and drink from the river. When I asked if that was a safe thing to do, he said, "I've been drinking from the river all my life. Why stop now?"

We visited often with Connie and Dena. They knew how much we wanted to get into ranching on our own. When the folks who normally custom-hayed for them weren't available one year, Hansens asked if we'd like to take on the project. What an opportunity! Suddenly we had to learn about ditches, irrigation, and the operation of some ancient haying equipment. This led to our leasing their ranch for a ridiculously low price, actually almost nothing, perhaps because they were so fond of the kids and wanted to help with their "ranch education." Our summer days filled to exploding.

At first, while Roy learned from Connie how to manage water-gates to irrigate the hayfields, the kids played along the river and tried fishing (rarely successfully). Or they watched the water gradually creep along, turn into the proper channels, and then fill the ditches. Later in the summer, after Roy had mowed the fields, they used old-fashioned wooden hay-forks to help gather and add to the windrows what the old dump rake missed. Sam helped fork the loose hay onto the wagon, and then the kids rode in the hay back to the barn.

Now with the availability of pasture on the Hansen place after the hay was in that fall, we managed a loan to buy twenty head of Simmental-cross cattle. Of course, we'd have to find them other pasture next spring when the hay meadows started growing, but we could worry about that next year. We began to feel like ranchers.

The Hansens had retired from active ranching many years earlier, and Connie had then worked for the Wyoming

Highway Department. They bought a small house in Laramie to make it easier for him to get to work, and now, especially in winter, they spent part of their time in town, part at their ranch. Their ancient pinto mare, Dixie, was living out her days on the ranch and needed a companion. When we learned that a neighbor up the river had "outgrown" a gentle, mature palomino, we were able to buy her. Cindy joined Dixie on the Hansen place. The kids were all overjoyed, especially Jenny. Our very own horse!

Then a friend, whose professor husband had acquired a long-term entomological project in Puerto Rico, needed a place for her two-year-old Quarter horse, Kneenowwa. She wanted me to train the young gelding to ride while she was away in the Caribbean. Now I could put into practice all I'd been learning from Ellie, and Kneenowwa's pasture rent provided a bit of income besides. To add another happy note, he came with saddle, bridle, halter, and lead rope. The kids and I spent as much time at the Hansen place as possible.

When the kids went back to school in the fall, my days formed into a new pattern. I wrote about it to my mom:

After the kids leave on the bus, Peggy and I drive up to Woods Landing, then follow a dirt lane up a hill, and down and through a small canyon and around a bend into the Hansen place. If the weather's okay we can drive by the house and up the hill to the lock gate, but if it's too snowy, we park by the house and walk up. At this point, Buster, a black Lab

*belonging to some neighbors back down the road, runs up to
say hello. He and Peggy kiss and then look for rabbits to chase.
Deer might be behind the house or anywhere up the hill, or
in the draw, or on the next hill—they watch us for a minute
but aren't in the least bothered.*

*If the horses aren't waiting by the pasture gate, I unlock the
door to the tackroom/grainroom, get halters, and walk out
to find them. They want to be caught since it means grain, so
no trouble there. Tie them at the manger in their own places.
Then go dish up the grain into their private pans and take
that out. While they're eating, check feet or curry and brush
or whatever.*

Winter made the process more complicated. While the
horses ate their grain, I forked last summer's sweet-smelling
hay from the crib into their manger. When they were finished,
I took off the halters. Dixie first, then Kneenowwa, and
Cindy last, because Cindy always figured I gave the best hay
to somebody else. Soon as she was loose, she'd ram over to
Kneenowwa and push him out of the way. He'd go to her
hay then and everybody was happy. She reminded me of
Toots. Sweet as Cindy generally was with people, she quickly
established herself as boss when it came to other horses.

Then came the big job, heading down the steep hill to
break open a hole in the frozen water gap, where the fence
extended into the river, making a place for livestock to drink.
We kept an ax and shovel by the gap fence. While I worked

on this sometimes-lengthy project, Peggy investigated the multitude of animal tracks or was entertained by a couple of cheeky squirrels.

I wrote home:

The river is fascinating—it rises and falls during the winter sometimes as much as a couple of feet. Sometimes it freezes over when high, and then drops, so that the water level is a foot or more below the ice. Or it can freeze over low, and then water bubbles up somewhere and runs over the top of the ice. Tricky for making the water gap safe and convenient for horses to drink from. Anyway, the river's always changing—ice caving in, new channels opening.

After checking the salt block and sometimes wiring up a new top pole on the old, rotting buck fence (on weekends, we spent a *lot* of time fixing fence around the place), I usually had to rush home, change clothes, and head in to work at the university. But if it wasn't one of my workdays, I stopped at the house to visit with Connie and Dena and listen to their stories of characters and events of the past.

※ ৴ ※ ৴ ※ ৴ ※

At school, the first major celebration of the school year was Halloween. The party at school needed community participation and donations—apples for the bobbing tub, pumpkins, corn shocks, colorful clusters of Indian corn ears, and bales of hay for decoration. Parents festooned the ceiling with crepe paper streamers in black and orange and created a haunted house with peeled-grape eyeballs, slimy detached hands, hanging skeletons, spiders in cheesecloth webs, eerie moans, and rattling chains.

Costumes were the big challenge. Some mothers sewed dazzling princess outfits or complicated animals, ogres, or Wizard-of-Oz creations. Easily fashioned cowboys, ghosts, and scarecrows abounded, and we sometimes resorted to those options. One year, Fred went as a witch, his favorite of all costumes because no one recognized him. They thought he was Jenny.

But we were limited by my lack of sewing skills. For costume creation, we relied on ingenuity, using cardboard boxes, old sheets and clothes, poster board, hay, crayons, paints and markers, glue, tape, and staples to make a sandwich-board playing card, whatever any of us could think of. Frank once won a prize as a railroad engineer, Sam as a Persian rug merchant.

"Mommy," Jenny said. "I want to be a Cinderella princess with a long, sparkling dress and glass slippers and a pumpkin coach."

"Umm, I'm not sure how to make that. Can you think of something else?"

"I could be a ballerina, with pointy shoes and a stick-out skirt!"

"Uh, let's go back to Cinderella. How about the raggedy version? We could give you a scrub brush and a bucket," I suggested brightly.

"I don't want raggedy. Maybe I could be a book."

"A book?"

"With a Cinderella cover," she enthused.

"That might work. We've got some poster board, and you could draw the cover the way you want it. Let's see, we could put in a few pages. . . . " Now that my imagination was roaming in more familiar territory, I could see a number of possibilities for a sandwich-board book, and Jenny took up the plan happily.

This worked, and we launched into production.

Roy had no more inclination to dress up than I did, but he was always on the lookout for what he considered the perfect Halloween disguise.

"Did you find my costume yet?"

"What?"

"You know. A Nixon mask." Rubbery, real-looking masks were coming into favor in the stores, and while vampires and movie stars filled the shelves, we never found a Nixon image. Still, Roy loved Halloween, both the party at school and individual trick-or-treating. He'd gather our kids and others, usually Lois from the neighboring ranch and George from next door at Ellie's, and drive the gang around the far-flung ranches to collect their loot. I loved him doing this. It gave me "time off" to catch up on home chores (I was always behind), or on due-tomorrow book reviews, or even to just put my feet up.

Another regular fall event was the annual pancake supper in support of our local volunteer fire department—one truck and all the men in the area. The meal consisted of pancakes (all you could eat) and ham, served with Emma's homemade chokecherry and wild berry syrups. Everyone pitched in. We expected, and usually had, a large turnout from Laramie, Woods Landing, Fox Park, and around the countryside.

One year, I spent much of the day helping set up tables and chairs with Emma and a few other ladies, as well as driving the twenty miles to town for last-minute items and to make a final sweep of merchants for donated door prizes. Fred once won a door prize that delighted him as much as it distressed most everyone else: two cans of kerosene. To his disappointment, he was finally persuaded to give up this treasure and trade with Chuck for an attractive wooden checkerboard, dark and light squares of wood, put together with Chuck's prized glue gun.

Several of us started flipping flapjacks at five in the after-noon and kept right on flipping until 8:30. Sam and other upper class kids bussed tables, and Roy took his turn washing dishes. Standing for hours in the steaming, crowded kitchen, I wondered at one point what in the world I was doing. How had I gotten *here,* in the midst of cacophony and bustle, all of us tripping over one another? I cherished the quiet of early mornings when I could write because I could really think, or when the dog and I could sit on the front step, listen to the birds, and watch the crescendo of sunrise. I loved the solitude of resting by the river, of silencing the frustrating thoughts of daily obligations, of listening instead to the inspiration that flowed around me from the river, the trees, and the clouds—those moments when I could be Me, Writer, instead of that other person: Mother, Wife, Chauffeur, Cook, Teacher, Janitor, Neighbor, and on and on.

And then . . . wait a minute, wait a minute! Inner dawn burst and glowed. This was what I wanted, wasn't it? This belonging? To be a part, an accepted, needed part, of the community? My family, all these families, these neighbors, working together—working joyfully—for a cause that might appear insignificant in the eyes of the world, but here and now was mighty and meaningful?

I glanced at the woman serving up slices of ham, the one who last year had been looking for people her own age to be friends with. Her face was flushed, but she seemed content. For now, at least, we were all embraced in community.

I kept flipping flapjacks with renewed energy, no longer on grumpy automatic pilot. My Hermit-Writer fantasies could wait.

MA, YOU'RE NOT
GOING TO LIKE THIS

Ice rimed the edges of the river rocks and began its slow creep out across the water until it shrouded the river. When the crust became solid, 4-H meetings were planned at a ranch up the river above Jelm where the ice was especially thick and smooth, so that kids and adults could go ice skating, or sliding, if skates were unavailable. The scene reminded me of a Brueghel painting transposed into a woodsy Wyoming setting.

But I was always a little concerned about the ice. A few years earlier, when we'd had a family excursion, walking through the fields up to Ellie's, we had to cross the frozen river. Roy led our single-file march, testing the ice. Sam wandered off-course from the route laid by Roy. A crash, a shout, and there he was in the river! Roy made a dashing rescue, and we hurried on to Ellie's to dry them both out by the stove.

※ ∕ ※ ∕ ※ ∕ ※

In the first storm of our first year in the cabin, I wrote to my parents:

This house, despite its little inconveniences, is the solidest I've ever been in. It's absolutely creakless in the most howling gale, and there's not a saggy or squeaky floorboard in the place. Really comfortable and tight. Even the privy, lit and warmed with kerosene lanterns, is quite picturesque.

While intended to assure my folks that we weren't perishing in a miserable hut, wrapped in blankets and huddled around a bonfire in the middle of the living room, the description remained true enough, and for that I was everlastingly grateful.

Still, among the cabin's "little inconveniences," a new cold-weather problem emerged that added to the everyday difficulties. The drainpipe froze. Chuck had fit the drain under the sink into a pipe that exited through a pre-existing hole in the wall out into the yard. We'd patched the hole around the pipe as best we could, and insulated the patch with rags. The boys found some old pipe to extend the drain further away from the cabin, which lessened its slope. This gravity-feed system worked well enough in warm weather, but iced up quickly in the cold, especially since, although a foot or so above the floor of the cabinet, the pipe emerged from the outside cabin wall four feet above the ground. We detached the extension. Even so, the bare drainpipe froze in a blink there on the north side of the house.

We had our choice of remedies. We could detach the pipe under the sink and let the water drain into a bucket placed under the sink, but then we'd have to carry it outside to empty. This meant keeping a careful eye to avoid overfilling and splashing water around the kitchen. Choice number two was to thaw the drain.

Fred and I would gather sticks and small chunks of firewood to build a fire outside under the pipe. This had its drawbacks. For one thing, we had to build the fire far enough out to avoid igniting the cabin. The general idea was to melt the ice at the end of the pipe (not too difficult), thereby heating the pipe enough to warm its way back toward the house, gradually thawing the whole line. If you haven't tried this for yourself, you might not realize how long it can take. Sometimes tears of frustration froze on my face while my fingers grew numb and Fred groaned and complained.

When the drainpipe was finally clear, I ran inside to wash all the stacked and waiting dishes and do other chores that required water coming in and going out (washing my hair, perhaps) before everything froze up again.

I suppose I grumbled about this sort of activity on occasion, especially if I arrived late and frazzled at some function. Once I muttered about it to an acquaintance sitting next to me, by way of excuse for my late arrival.

"Why don't you just leave?" she asked. "What do you care about this country stuff?"

I stared. She was serious and continued, "Let your husband take care of it. Just leave him and move to town."

Shocked, I realized maybe wallowing around in a blizzard trying to light a fire in the snow did sound pretty stupid to someone else. In fact, I admitted to myself, I'd been exaggerating a bit for effect, already seeing the absurdity and humor of the situation. But leave my husband? Move to town? Had I sounded *that* put upon?

The questions pulled me up short. Was I feeling sorry for myself? Okay, maybe so, but not to the point of bemoaning my fate or blaming Roy or anyone else for choices I'd made. I *wanted* to live in the country, and the tradeoffs I'd made were more than worth the hardships. Roy and I had entered this project together, and if it wasn't working out quite the way I'd envisioned, I still wanted to work our way *through* the problems, not abandon ship.

Lesson learned: quitcher bellyaching! To anyone else, anyway. If I felt like indulging myself sometimes just to let off steam, so be it. But as my uncle's father, an old upstate New York dairy farmer, used to say, "Might as well laugh as cry." Most of the time, I did.

※ ✎ ※ ✎ ※ ✎ ※

Now that we had cows to feed, living at the cabin, five miles from our ranching operations at the Hansen place, had its drawbacks. For one thing, we had no stock trailer, so had to trail our cows along the highway when we moved them. If our horses were at one place and we wanted them at the other, we had to ride them back and forth. As the kids gained skill in their riding, we needed another horse or two so that they could help with the cows. This led to finding Rex, a great sweetheart of a horse who somehow became mine.

His parentage was obscure, but must have included Percheron and Appaloosa blood to account for his size, his sunny color, and the dapples that faded away under his heavy winter coat. His gait was so smooth, so comfortable to ride, I forgave his tendency toward flightiness. He could shy at anything in a great sideways leap that shot him eight feet to one side or the other in an instant. This might have unseated me easily except that in his smoothness he somehow kept me aboard, although on one occasion he twirled so fast my glasses sailed off into the brush and I had to paw around in a blur for ten minutes to find them.

One day, riding Rex with young Kneenowwa on a lead, I was bringing home two heifers that were due to calve. We wanted to keep a close eye on them in the corrals by the cabin.

I'd dreamed about this kind of thing years ago, dreamed of dashing across the open prairie on a fiery steed, of feeling strong muscles rippling beneath me and the brush of mane against my hand, of hearing the rhythmic pound of hoofbeats, smelling the heavenly scent of horseflesh. And here I was, thirty-some years later, actually living the dream. Sort of. I discovered that a dream can fall a bit short when pared down to the bones of reality.

For one thing, my dream took place under a blue sky, picturesquely studded with puffy clouds. The only wind in my dream was generated by my thundering passage or else a friendly breeze that energized and delighted. Today the wind howled. Temperatures dropped well below freezing. Snow pellets built into drifts where my thighs pressed against the saddle. I'd lost feeling in my toes, and my fingers were going fast. The open prairie had morphed into a borrow pit between the highway and a barbed wire fence. Galloping, even if I'd been so inclined, was impossible because of the need to move the cows at a gentle pace. And I wanted to avoid exciting the young horse, to say nothing of keeping Rex, already nervous in the wind-driven buckshot snow, from losing his cool— and me—altogether.

The dream never encountered an obstacle or questioned the harmonious togetherness of horse and rider. Now I could see a semi-truck coming toward us on the highway, throwing up clouds of snow. I tried to settle even deeper into the saddle and spoke soothingly to Rex in psalms and hymns, hoping to impress him with the absolute safety and control of the situation. No need to worry, or panic, or shy into either the fence or the highway. The semi didn't slow down or pull to the other side of the road. No. As it came upon us, I could see the driver's grinning face just an instant before he leaned on his air horn.

Actually, as far as dreams went, I got the "fiery steed" part right. When Vesuvius quit erupting and the snow-ash settled, I was grateful to find myself still on Rex. A kind of well-what-do-you-know! moment. Though somewhat entangled with Kneenowwa's lead rope, we happily had not encountered the barbed wire fence. I reached up and felt my glasses on my face where they belonged. I spied the heifers way up ahead, slowing to a trot, still aimed in the right direction. My heart was beating like a jackhammer, but that was probably good, keeping the blood circulating through the benumbed fingers of my rein hand. The sound of the receding semi disappeared into the wind.

✳ ⸝ ✳ ⸝ ✳ ⸝ ✳

After Thanksgiving, everyone's attention turned to Christmas, and the kids had school projects to consider, making gifts for parents and other family members. These varied with age group and often involved Chuck's help in providing wood (paid for by the parents), cut into pattern-blanks from which the kids constructed racks to hold keys, a broom, mail, scarves, or caps. The kids carefully sanded and stained or varnished the wood and presented the final product with pride. Sam's wall sconce hangs in my kitchen today. The younger kids made tree ornaments from colored pipe cleaners, cotton balls, and paper, or they fashioned pencil holders from an empty can, around which they pasted popsicle sticks, then decorated with felt cut-out designs, paint, and ribbon.

And then came the Christmas program. Skits, recitations, carols in chorus or solo, every kid took part. Presenting the Christmas story was obligatory, either as a tableau or a skit. One of the older kids read from Luke in the King James Bible. Costumes for Mary, Joseph, kings, and shepherds were easy enough, utilizing a lot of bathrobes, tablecloths, and towels, but the angels were trickier because of wings and halos. Dena helped me fashion a halo and wings for Jenny out of wire frames covered with pastel tissue-paper—very effective, but fragile and a bit difficult to keep from tilting askew, giving a rakish or slightly tipsy effect to the angel.

Sam brought home a note from his teacher and looked worried when he handed it to me. "Ma, I don't think you're going to like this very much."

Casually hand-written, it read: "Sam is to be Santa Claus for one skit. Please sew up a costume for him by Friday."

This arrived on a day when stove, pitcher pump, drain, cats, and snowdrifts had all conspired against me in various ways, and the note presented the last straw. I blew my stack by return note. I ranted on about stereotypes: just because I was a mother, or just because I lived in the country, did that mean I could sew? Did it mean that even if I *could* sew, I had time to drop everything and whip out a costume in five minutes? Or that I had the wherewithal to buy, or materials on hand to produce, a Santa suit, hat, beard, etc.? And why wouldn't a teacher ask about this to begin with instead of just assuming. . . .

I'm afraid there may have been several pages of this potent venting, which eventually wound down with assurances that I would be glad to help in some way. Not sewing, but maybe with lettering, poster-making, or typing.

My rant produced a return letter from the teacher, perhaps calculated to mollify me, as well as to restore a reasonable parent-teacher relationship:

Dear Mrs. Collier,

The school has a Santa Claus costume, and I apologize for not looking into this before. Frank has some summaries to write for Social Studies, as well as his Math. He is doing well in other subjects, and is doing especially well in Reading.

I want you to know that Sam has done something that has both surprised and thrilled me. I had chosen Sam for the editor of the December newspaper, but I was really doubtful about whether we would be able to manage a paper this month with the plays and all the things there are to do, making gifts, etc. Usually I end up making assignments, proof-reading, and the rest, so you can imagine how I felt when I saw that Sam, under his own initiative, had thought up the assignments, handed them out, and set his own deadline for having them handed in. This is what I call accepting responsibility, and it is a really sure sign of maturity. This is a great help to me, and I'm sure our December paper will be one of the best.

If you can type, that is a sewingless way to help me.

Instantly I fell in love with the woman. I did do a lot of typing for her, and she began taking guitar lessons from me.

At home as elsewhere, Christmas meant lights and decorations, and of course a tree. Most years, this required heading up into the Medicine Bow National Forest with ax and hand saw, a permit, and all of us suitably attired in winter outfits, boots, mittens, scarves and so on, and snacks or a picnic lunch.

The adventure started out cheerfully. We found a place to park where pristine snow indicated that the spot hadn't already been invaded by other tree hunters, and tumbled out of the pickup. The day fairly crackled with crisp beauty: a brilliant blue overhead, snow-sparkle diamonds flashing on tree limbs, the fresh, pungent scent of pine and spruce. Radiating exuberance, Roy and Peggy plunged into the forest. The rest of us followed, puffing steamy breath into the chill air. Sometimes we walked in Roy's tracks where he had already broken a trail through deep drifts. I hoped we'd accomplish our purpose fairly quickly, before cold and fatigue could turn the joy of wilderness exploration into a painful chore.

The problem was finding the perfect tree. Roy was very specific about this. No short, fat, bushy pines. There wasn't room in the house, for one thing. Roy's aesthetic sense required a tall, graceful tree—full, symmetrical, preferably a short-needled fir. Long pine needles interfered with exact placement of the lights.

Sam ran through a drift to a perfectly shaped young tree. Just right, I thought. Wonderful! And so soon! "Hey, Pa!" he called. "Here's a good one!"

Roy took the opportunity to expound on forest management. "It's all by itself and could grow into a beautiful big tree. We need to find one in a group that needs thinning. Then cutting one will help the other trees get more light and branch out into a better shape."

Premonition grew as we continued tramping through the snow. This was not to be a speedy accomplishment. Jenny whined. "I'm co-o-o-ld!"

"Hey, we're just getting started," I said with a lilt to my voice, as though that would warm her up.

Frank shouted, pointing. "Over there!"

Roy countered, "That one has a gap in its branches, Franker. We can find something better."

By this time I was seriously on the lookout. I wanted to wrap this up while we were still having fun. I spotted a tree about the right size at the edge of a group. It looked full and shapely, and the other trees' habitat would be improved by our cutting it. "There!" I said. "That's a beautiful tree. My toes are cold. Let's take it."

"Too bushy. Besides, it's a pine." Roy's fingers, toes, and ears were as impervious to cold as his temperament was to our growing despair. He attributed to us the same joy of the quest he experienced, so why hurry?

Jenny congealed to a stop, tears in her eyes. "I'm fro-o-o-zen! I want to go home."

I yelled to Roy as he forged ahead. "Do you see something we can take? Anything? The kids are freezing up!"

"Not yet," he called back cheerfully.

"Well, for heaven's sake, cut *something!* Jenny and I are going back to the truck."

Fred was torn between following the others and warming up, but only for a moment. He yelled, "Hey, Ma, wait for me!"

Back in the pickup I ran the heater for a while and wrapped the two kids in the blankets previous experience had taught me we'd need. We nibbled snacks. We told each other stories. We napped. Eventually, nearing sundown, the others dragged in our tree, Roy and Peggy still sprightly, Sam and Frank glum and grumpy. The tree had one flat side: not a serious defect, since that side could be set against the wall.

Too late to set up the tree when we got home. In fact, it was several days before Roy could get to it. First, of course, I had to find the stand, which I knew I'd put away last year in the bottom of one of the boxes of lights—which meant finding the boxes. Invariably they were buried deep in the stacks still piled in the porch, probably under Hopelessly Miscellaneous. Once I found them, we set all the Christmas ornament boxes in the middle of the living room floor and walked around them for days.

Roy then had to cut the base of the trunk perfectly level so that the tree would stand solidly upright. This was especially important because Toots like to spring into the tree as soon as it was up and set it rocking. I remembered Christmas back when my brother and I were kids. My father always bought a huge, bushy tree, even if he had to cut off the top third to get it into the house, where it spread like a miniature forest on one side of the living room. Roy would never cut the top of the tree, as doing so would spoil its taper. He sawed off the base half-inch by half-inch until the tree fit, with room for a light and an angel perched on the very tip.

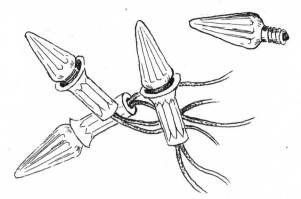

The kids dug through the ornaments.

"I like this one. Can I hang it up now?"

"I want to hang this one. Where are the hanger-things?"

"Why can't I put this up?"

"I have to get the lights up first," Roy said patiently, gradually untangling strings of bulbs. "Otherwise the ornaments might fall and break."

"Come on, kids," I said with semblance of cheer. "Let's make some paper chains. I'll clear a spot on the kitchen table."

Jenny went to work cutting strips of red and green construction paper, which Frank and Fred glued or taped into chains. "I'll make snowflakes," Sam said, folding squares of paper into sixths and cutting out designs. Unfolded, the "snowflakes" looked pretty festive, especially when hung on the paper chains, which soon festooned most of the house.

Frank tried making snowflakes, but when he unfolded his paper, it all fell apart. "Ma, this doesn't work! Let's do something else. I want to hang ornaments."

"Here are some colored pipe cleaners," I said. "Maybe you can fold these into bows or candy canes."

"Then can I hang them up?"

"Where are the Christmas candles? Can we set up the candles?" More digging through boxes, more strewing stuff around the floor. Herbert found a loose ornament to bat around. Fred found the little green pine-tree-shaped candles, and Jenny unearthed the antique skating Santa figure. "Where are the cotton balls?" They began constructing a winter scene on the edge of a bookshelf.

Unfortunately, none of this took as much time as necessary. "Roy, are you about ready?"

"Not yet." He loved setting up the lights. Along with our newer purchases, we had strings gleaned from our folks, old-fashioned lights where if one bulb went out, the whole string was dark. The bad bulb had to be found by trial and error. Roy was especially fond of these because of their fluted sides and slender, graceful shape, which he considered far more pleasing than the newer squatty design.

"You've got all the strings on now. Can't the kids start hanging ornaments?"

"I've got to get the colors right." He plugged in the wires, and some of the bulbs lit up. "Once I find the bad bulb, I'll work on the colors." He always arranged the lights in rainbow sequence with one white bulb at the top, then descending layers of red, orange, yellow, green, blue, and purple, with a bottom row of bubble lights.

At last the kids and I could begin hanging ornaments, the smallest balls on the upper branches, gradually increasing in size going down. Roy was in charge of placing the family relics, like the Santa head and lovely silver and blue pinecones, near the top where they'd be safe. By this time, of course, the kids were all frantic to get their first ornaments on the tree, then rush to grab another.

"Take it easy! Take your time!" Roy's words of caution were invariably punctuated with a crash, followed by wails and tiresome waits to sweep up the broken glass.

Jenny hung some jingle bells on a low branch for Herbert to bat at without expending too much energy while I looked around to try to find Toots. I knew she wouldn't wait long before adding her two cents worth.

Just too late, I saw her crouched to spring. "Watch out!" I yelled.

She launched herself into the tree a little above the mid-point and hung on as it started to sway dangerously. "Nixon!" Roy made a grab and steadied the tree while Toots dislodged a ball and watched it bounce through the branches and shatter on the floor. She apparently thought this was the point of the whole operation. Why else would people bring a tree into the house?

"Kids, bring some blankets to cushion under the tree after I clean this up. Sam, can you find the string and some tacks? Watch out now!. Don't step on the broken glass."

Roy tethered the tree to the wall in a couple of places to make sure it wouldn't fall. As the excitement wound down, we added tinsel, ropes of glitter, pipe-cleaner wreaths, and whatever else suited our fancy, then stood back to admire our work. Despite the delays, frustrations, and disturbances, it was basically a happy event. More than a Christmas tree, the result was a family art project.

At last we arranged the packages under the bottom branches. Grandparents shipped cartons tightly packed with beautifully wrapped gifts. The wrappings on my artist grandfather's presents were art objects of design in paper, paint, ribbon, and colored tape, almost too pretty to open (unless you were a kid). We learned right away that Peggy's wrapped gift couldn't be placed under the tree until the last minute. Her nose quickly detected the thinly disguised, large dog biscuit, and she didn't fiddle around waiting for permission to tear through the paper.

Instead of using ready-made gift cards, Roy designed his own, always accompanied by his little drawings. One Christmas I received a pair of warm socks with the tag, *"Merry Christmas! To Gaysey: For the feet I love to warm (in July). Love, Roy (wrapped the way Nana mended them)."* This last was in reference to my grandmother, as sewing-challenged as I, who "darned" Pappy's socks by running a thread around the hole and pulling it up tight, thereby closing the hole and rendering the sock unfit to wear. Often Roy's gifts were presented to us as from the pets, "signed" with pawprints or dog and cat faces.

For our anniversary two days later, he gave me a box of chocolates adorned with:

Well 12 years have come to a close,
But my fondness for you still daily grows—
Ever since that great day in Brewster [N.Y., where we
    spent our wedding night]
When I became your devoted booster.

This little gift, to an angel from a snake,
Is an infinitesimal part of what you should partake.
And as for a gift from you to me, Little Mouse,
Please rescue me from that danged "open house."

The last line referred to a dress-up affair we were supposed to attend.

Sometimes on Christmas Eve, folks got together to go caroling, stopping from ranch to ranch along the river. We kept popcorn and cocoa hot and invited everyone in to admire our tree.

Christmas Day began early, the rule being that no one could open a present until everyone was there to watch, and then only one present could be opened at a time, so everyone could admire and appreciate both gift and giver. Roy loved this rule. It could drag out the unveiling process for hours. I once tried requiring a thank-you note to be written before going on to the next present, but this proved ridiculous and was soon abandoned. The biggest problem was getting Roy up early enough to satisfy everyone else, especially since he had probably stayed up most of the night rearranging light bulbs and shifting ornaments an inch this way or that to achieve aesthetic perfection. The best solution seemed to be for him to just stay up until the gifts were open. He could crump out later.

Some folks take their tree down pretty quickly after Christmas Day, certainly by New Year's. They're the folks who managed to get it up and decorated weeks ahead of time. Since we never finished decorating until the last minute, and often not even then, we weren't in a rush to take it down. In fact, Roy was loath to take down the tree at all. All that work shouldn't be dispatched until thoroughly, and at length, appreciated. This protracted Christmas season was okay for a while. But even with careful nurture, the tree dried and began losing its needles. I sometimes had Poe-like visions of what the house would look like with years of Christmas trees crammed into the living room in progressive stages of gruesome disintegration. I finally put my foot down and established a new rule: the Christmas tree had to come down by Valentine's Day.

Roy exulted in admiring the tree's beauty. Instead of going to bed at night, he'd turn off all the house lights and lie on the couch so he could look at the tree. He'd fall asleep there, his face multi-colored in the glow of the lights, a smile on his lips, and Herbert curled on his stomach.

HEY, HERBERT TIPPED OVER
THE GAME BOARD

WINTER STORMS in the high country of the Laramie Valley could be cold and snowy, but the big factor was always wind. One night, I heard it while lying in bed and wondered if all the clothes would blow off the line. They didn't. I brought them in just after noon, still frozen into boards. Finally, with a little thawing and considerable effort, I bent them over clothes bars and chairs to continue thawing.

The wind rolled the snow into pellets that piled up into stiff, compact drifts where you didn't want them (usually in the roads) and where they became nearly impenetrable. On the west side of the schoolyard, ranchers had built a windbreak of slabs, the bark-covered edges trimmed from logs at the sawmill. This fence accumulated eight-foot drifts that made gigantic snow-slides for the kids.

Wind-whipped snow produced ground blizzards on the two-lane highway, forming shifting crisscross patterns that mesmerized eyes and mind. This was a normal condition on the Laramie plains, an expected inconvenience. But sometimes on my twenty-five-mile commute when I worked in town, the snow whipped up into a froth, a whiteout, that made driving close to impossible. Then I was afraid to keep going and equally afraid to stop for fear someone was coming along behind me. I tried to pull over onto the shoulder, which in some places was nonexistent, gauging my way by the feel of the right tires. More than once, a semi roared around me full speed, churning the snow-froth into even wilder frenzy. In the midst of my outrage, I realized that, with his head up there above the maelstrom, the driver could probably see just fine. Maybe the sun was even shining and the tops of cars appeared to him as black turtle shells floating in a white sea.

Just like my life. I was living in a ground-blizzard of busyness, its ever-shifting crosscurrents occasionally flaring up into clouds of confusion. Two things helped me rise above the turmoil, allowing me a brief respite to orient myself and make sure I was on the right path, before dipping again below the surface. My early-morning spiritual reading gave me a rod and staff to lean on as I stumbled through the misty valley of the day. And second, my trips to the river, the soothing grandmother, offered comfort that promised strength and purpose. Somehow this cabin experience was requiring more grit and courage than I had ever imagined. The river reminded me with her sound and scent, even when bubbling beneath a cloak of ice, of the table of beauty and provision spread before me.

I came to value the river deeply—and the wind a bit less—as metaphors for my life. When I had first thought of the river in this context, I considered it too confined, its course too predetermined, to appeal to me. I loved the freedom and frolic of the wind, its ability to switch directions and change speeds on a whim, to sustain the glide of hawk or eagle, to toss up leaves and feathers. And I still loved it. But Wyoming's wind had exposed me to its rougher nature, its fierce insistence on having its own way, on pushing life into rock-strewn paths, to tossing *me* along with the leaves.

I was learning that life does have boundaries, that it needs some measure of control; that when we set a course, we must follow it—unless forced to portage cross-country over rough territory, leaving the life-sustaining waters behind. I wasn't ready to do that. Instead, the river was showing me gentle dependability, strength, and quiet expectation. Where once I'd looked for the excitement of adventure, now I discovered the joy of quiet acceptance, not the drudgery or boredom of resignation, but rather the blossoming of a deeper understanding of the beauty I already knew was part of the land.

Where the wind represented suggestion and opportunity, the river opened to me both nourishment and promise. I learned to appreciate what I had instead of looking for something more, something else. Sometimes that was hard in the midst of knock-down-cold winter, but for the most part it shone through.

✳ ↝ ✳ ↝ ✳ ↝ ✳

County plows did their best to clear the highways. Ranchers used their tractors with plow attachments to open a way through their fields to feed hay to their livestock. After that they cleared a path through the back roads. In the meantime, we shoveled. And shoveled. Returning from town one night after a dog-training class that Ellie taught, she and I had to dig most of our way in from the highway. The storm had intensified while we were gone and was now blowing with blinding fury. We had two shovels, and we each jumped out, scooped a few feet ahead, jumped back in the car and drove into the cleared tracks, then jumped out again to shovel more as the roaring wind filled in behind us. It was after midnight when we got home.

Sometimes the school bus got stuck in the drifts and the shovelings of Chuck and the older boys couldn't dig it out. There were no cell phones then, so families watched the clock. They knew when the bus was due, and if it was late, someone drove a tractor to find it and pull it free. Once in a while, Chuck would leave Lois and the other kids on the route with us, where they'd be warm and dry, maybe even fed with cocoa and popcorn, until the ranchers could get through to pick them up. In storms, the electricity might go off for several hours, even days, at a time. For us, this presented only a minor inconvenience. We had our kerosene lamps, and anything in the refrigerator could simply be set outside in a snow bank. Once, we received a call from the wealthy new neighbors down the road.

"Hi there. Are you keeping warm?"

"You bet," I said. "We have fires blazing away in both our stoves and the house is toasty."

"Well, I wonder if we could bring the kids up for a while. They're getting pretty cold. We remodeled and put in all-electric heating. We plan to get a wood stove too but don't have it in yet."

"Why, of course!" I gushed. Such exquisite gratification! What a rare pleasure! Oh Lord, forgive my smugness! (But I didn't berate myself too much.)

Sometimes the phone went out. If the electricity was off, too, we settled into cozy isolation in the soft glow of the kerosene lamps. We had a battery-powered radio that sometimes worked, and we could listen to school closings, road closings, official pleas not to venture out in the storm, and reports of needed or achieved rescues of various kinds.

Kids bundled up for trips to the privy or to bring in more wood.

"Try to get more snow off the wood outside before you bring it all in," I suggested.

"Well, I swept it," Sam said. "And I swept off Frank, too." I wouldn't have known by the amount of snow that accompanied them inside. They hung coats, caps, and scarves on hooks and piled their boots by the door.

We set up an old card table in the living room, and the kids argued over the pile of board games until deciding on Monopoly or Careers or Chinese checkers. We set the lamps in the best locations for seeing the game or reading, if any of us were doing that.

Roy always cautioned, "Be careful! Don't bump the lamp!" I don't recall that we ever had a problem with this—certainly we never had a spill or fire.

The games started with great joy and enthusiasm, but after a while degenerated a bit, sometimes to tears though not often to the point of blood.

"Mommy, do you know what Sam did?"

"Cheater!"

"Hey ma, can you get Herbert? He's in the middle of the board."

Sometimes two kids retreated into a thoughtful game of chess, played on Fred's door-prize chessboard. If Roy was home, he often played with them, especially chess. And he loved to play Monopoly; but this wasn't always fondly received, as he had a cutthroat desire to play until no one else had a single house or dollar left. He'd even try to loan money to the other players in order to drag the game out longer, to his pleasure and everyone else's misery. When we all played a game together, we usually opted for Yahtzee. One night Roy and Jenny built a wooden chair for her Raggedy Ann doll.

The wind whistled in the chimney, and snow pellets rattled against the windows. Toots curled up with Peggy in front of the kitchen stove. Herbert kept spreading himself out on the game board, and the other cats and kittens living with us at the moment tucked themselves into whatever laps or pillows they could find.

If Roy and I had wanted to live in, and let the kids experience, the past—the good Currier-and-Ives, Norman-Rockwell, Little-House-books past—we couldn't have come much closer than this.

✳ ↝ ✳ ↝ ✳ ↝ ✳

By mid-January, a long crack stretched up the middle of the river, an inch wide, and deep, deep down to the water. In one spot, I could look down eight inches or so through crystal-clear ice, but mostly milky-white prevailed. When Roy walked home one night, he heard three great cracks, like rifle shots, two upstream from the bridge and one down, as chunks of ice broke apart. In my diary, I recorded:

Feb. 10: You can hear the river again. A great chunk of ice dropped out of the middle of the channel, and other areas are breaking up. The nights have been cold, around ten degrees, but the days have warmed—snow melting, ground thawing. Everyone's holding their breath for the storm that's bound to come.

Spring was the time for wild storms to blow in suddenly when the weather was warm, the rangeland just greening, and a few tentative robins sang promise. Furious squalls might come in March or April, sometimes even May, great clouds boiling out of a blue-sky morning, temperature plummeting, snow swirling from nothing into a roaring sideways waterfall of white. These were the dangerous storms that trapped travelers and buried cattle and forced snow around window frames and doorjambs to form mounds of white on sills and carpets; storms you read about from pioneer days that froze children on their way home from country schools and let ranchers die trying to find their way from house to barn—storms to be respected.

Despite the vicious cavalry-and-saber attacks of the storms, spring foot-soldiered in, slow but steady, sometimes accompanied by a melodic Air Force of wild geese heading north. Migrating mallards by the thousand rested at ease on the river or nearby Sodergreen Lake. Grass pushed up, the blades holding as steady as lances through occasional two-inch blankets of snow that quickly melted. Dandelions polka-dotted the green with sunshine before changing into white helmets of fluff.

Calving and lambing kept ranchers busy round the clock, and often the storms turned routine two-hour checks of the birthing sheds into full-scale rescue operations. Home kitchens became maternity wards for fuzzy newborns whose mothers weren't quick enough to get them cleaned up and dried off before they froze in the snow and wind. Roy had plenty of work then, helping with these operations, feeding, mucking out sheds, or whatever was needed.

Every animal's survival was important, determining the ranchers' profit or loss for the year. With Ellie, survival of a foal was critical, since only a few were born each spring, each with—for registered Arabians—the potential value of thousands of dollars. She kept a close eye on her mares when their time was near. Sometimes she phoned me late at night to spell her or help with a potentially tricky birth—though when a situation looked too bad, she'd call out a vet from town.

One night, I went down to the barn around 10:30 to join Ellie, and we sat talking, waiting, chilly, but wrapped in the scent of horse and hay and old wood. The dim light cast by a single bulb threw shadows into the corners and highlighted the marks of ax and adz on the hewn logs. This seemed to be a female thing. Bill's temperament couldn't put up with waiting around, and Roy was either working elsewhere or sleeping his usual sleep of the dead. In the quiet night hours with the mare, my Peggy, and Ellie's Minx and Scamper, we girls talked intimately of our dreams, hopes, and disappointments. We shared a friendship that blessed us both and gathered in our furry companions.

Like the big house, the barn had been skillfully constructed with pegs, each beam and log perfectly squared and trimmed by the early Swedish settlers. The large stalls had originally boarded big freighter teams as they rested on the stage route from Laramie to North Park, Colorado. The mare, nervous and more used to the outdoors, kept trying to unhook the gate that confined her to the straw-padded stall. After she managed it once, Ellie tied the hook with baling twine. The mare paced, pawed, swung her head from side to side, and then stood stock still, head high, looking and listening as though something were up in the loft, making us as nervous as she was until we climbed up to check. Nothing there; she was listening to something beyond our ken.

We went into the house for a quick cup of coffee, then back out again to wait. The mare foaled around 2:00 in the morning—a filly, whose forehead bore the white design of a reverse question mark. Mama went right to cleaning up her baby, but because of the cold, we helped by rubbing with burlap sacks and towels. After a few staggering attempts, the foal stood, wobbling a bit, nuzzled under mama's belly, and, finally, with a few gentle nudges from the mare's nose, found the right spot and began sucking noisily. We left, smiling and profoundly happy.

After foals were on the ground, mares came into heat. Now was the time for Ellie's prize stallion to earn his keep. She had bought Fasaab in Utah where he'd been considered "over the hill," possibly still able to sire a colt or two, but otherwise not good for much. The magnificent black stallion had a stunning pedigree of Egyptian Arabian parentage, and from the moment he set foot on the ranch, he acted as though he was well aware of his kingly status. In the past he'd won many championships, and Ellie was sure that, even at his age, he could do so again.

Fasaab had spent the last year or more in a stall or small paddock; although he'd been well fed, he'd become fat, flabby, and dreadfully out of shape. Even breathing was a chore at this high altitude. I had the privilege of watching, even helping somewhat, as Ellie embarked on his transformation. At first she led him out across the river into the stubbled autumn hay meadow, walking and talking to him all the while, sharing her plans with him. He seemed to approve and cooperate with the effort. Sometimes Ellie had me ride him bareback as they walked, and after a while she began longeing him, first at a walk, then a trot. As his muscles rippled under me, it was like riding a thundercloud—smooth and soft but seething inside with power and spirit.

Gradually, as his condition improved, his energy returned. By spring, when grass began growing and they could no longer work on the meadow, Ellie rode him in the pasture north of the buildings while I gaped in admiration. Nostrils flaring, stepping high, he appeared to love the activity.

When one of Ellie's mares came into heat, I helped with "hand breeding." Fasaab and the mare were both too valuable to turn into a pen together and let them "have at it;" one could bite or kick and possibly damage the other. I held the mare on a lead by the tall corral fence while Ellie controlled the stallion on a long line, not sure at first how he might act after his long abstinence. The old horse turned out to be as much a gentleman, even at this exciting moment, as he had always been while Ellie groomed, walked, or rode him: *Don't worry. We royals know how to behave!*

I was glad the kids weren't around on this occasion, even though they were maturing and well aware of the facts of life when it came to cows and bulls. Fasaab performed with enthusiasm and power. However, perhaps his full strength hadn't quite returned. As he dismounted from the mare, he heaved a huge, groaning sigh of satisfaction, continued to sink back on his haunches, sat, and then fell over flat on his side. Ellie and I couldn't laugh too hard right then; it might have wounded his dignity.

Later that year, the kids and I babysat the other horses and did chores while Ellie took him to shows back in Utah and around the West. He wowed the crowds and again garnered championships.

Even as we continued to look for our own place, we were backing into ranching by acquiring livestock. We had big Rex, Cindy, our gentle palomino, and her foster-horse companion, Kneenowwa, along with a small herd of Simmental cows. Then came the sheep.

Norma, one of our neighbors, stopped by with a station-wagon-load of "bum"—orphan—lambs, hoping to find them a good home. Roy, of course, was ready to take on the whole crowd. I didn't think we were ready for any of them. The kids were ecstatic, all rushing to claim a lamb or two for their own.

"All right," I said at last and added with emphasis, "Four! One for each kid."

"Five," Roy said.

"Now look," I said. "*You* don't need an orphan lamb, and neither do I."

He'd been talking with Norma, and now he quietly said again, "Five." He nodded at Jenny, who was cuddling a wee lamb hardly as big as a cat. "That one is a triplet and very weak. Norma doesn't expect it to live."

Jenny and the tiny lamb were gazing into each other's eyes. She'd already named it Dinky. Oh brother, I thought. "Okay, five."

Norma gave us starter rations and some rubber nipples to attach to pop bottles to feed their formula. We set up a nest in a shed for the babies and gave Dinky a box in the kitchen by the stove. After a week or so of touch-and-go, with lots of love and cuddling from Jenny, Roy, and Peggy, Dinky perked up. She baa-ed to be fed. She attempted to jump out of her box.

"I don't think we need the box any more," Jenny said. "She always falls when she tries to jump out."

"Besides," Roy said, "she's found a better place to stay. Just look at that." Peggy was lying by the stove, and Dinky had curled up between her paws. Both dog and lamb seemed pleased with the arrangement. Sometimes Dinky climbed on top of the dog, turned around twice and nestled down on the warm fur. I was astonished at Peggy's tolerance for this, as the sharp little hooves danced over her body.

Lambs grow quickly, and it wasn't long before I considered using diapers. Besides, Dinky always seemed to be under foot, usually baaing for an extra feed. Her little hooves beat a rhythmic tattoo on the linoleum.

"I think Dinky's old enough to enjoy the outdoors," I said. "Why don't you take her out for a little while?"

Jenny agreed to this and carried Dinky outside where she started nibbling some new grass. She saw the other lambs and wandered over to touch noses.

"Maybe she'll be able to stay out with the others soon," Jenny said a bit sadly.

Sam opined, "Yes, I think that would be a good idea. She really should know she's a sheep and not a German shepherd." Soon the move was permanent.

The spring season signaled the end of hibernation for the wild critters. They emerged from their winter abodes hungry and grumpy. When I let Peggy out one night, she growled and tore off into the dark. She soon returned. We could smell her coming before we could see her. The skunk had let her have it right in the face, and she was a sight to look at, let alone smell. The time-honored stink remedy was a tomato-juice bath (nowadays vets usually recommend a baking soda-hydrogen peroxide mix). I was out of tomato juice, but had some puree, so I watered it down and doused her out on the steps, then brought her inside and dried her off in front of the stove. Everybody else went to bed and got far under the covers. Tomato juice helps but doesn't really complete the job. She stank for months, especially when wet.

Fred sometimes took personal offense at such assaults made against his friends, and he determined to do something about it. As a family, we enjoyed archery and had bows of various sizes and strengths. We set up several bales of hay, crayoned a bulls-eye target on cardboard or a paper sack, attached it to the bales, and shot from whatever distance suited our capabilities. Fred thought he could use his bow and arrow to get rid of the skunk, which apparently wanted to stick around. This was the kind of activity I usually found out about too late. Jenny was with him, but the older boys were off somewhere else, or they might have talked him out of the scheme.

I guess you could say the operation was a success, although the patient/victim didn't obligingly drop dead. Instead, it scrambled, arrow and all, into the crawl space under the house. Since the project couldn't be abandoned at that point, both for the skunk's sake and for ours, Fred crawled after it and managed to grab the arrow, then back out, pulling. The skunk came with the arrow and dealt his mortal revenge in Fred's face.

Our youngest had always been prone to nicknames, and for various obscure reasons was often called "Arch" (by Roy), "Wiggy" (me), and "Alphonse" or "Phonse-al" (Sam). This adventure earned him permanent sobriquet of "Skunk" from Jenny—a name she invariably used well into adulthood.

By May, spring weather was in full force. The river rushed, crowded the top of its banks or spilled over. The water table rose, low meadows flooded, and soon wild iris laid carpets of lavender between our cabin and the Pioneer Canal near the highway. Leaves budded and finally burst out on the trees. In the short time before the mosquitoes hatched out in profusion, and especially while the kids were still in school, I spent every spare moment down by the river, letting the roar of the water renew my vitality. More than once, feeling exhausted or even sickly, I'd stretch out on the grassy bank, fall asleep, and awake refreshed, ready to get back to work.

Most of the storms were over now, and while the high water limited some activities, it encouraged others. Sometimes kayakers would brave the torrent, come zooming down the river, and then have to make a quick side-pass for the shore to avoid getting their heads knocked off by the bridge. The wooden bridge crossed the river directly south of the dooryard between the big house and barn. The kids devised a "counting coup" game, where they'd lie on the weathered planks, each with a long stick, and try to tap whatever piece of driftwood or flotsam dashed by. One time, Sam counted over a hundred. I always hoped no kayakers would turn up on these occasions.

As the kids grew older, they spent more time fishing in the river. We enjoyed the trout they caught. Fishing had a deep tradition here. Neighbor Wes Johnson was a kid in the early 1900s. In his memoirs he wrote: "The Laramie River in those days was a fisherman's paradise. We learned to fish early. The fish were a big part of our summer diet and a great attraction to the sportsmen who came by livery rig or on bicycles."

And just as youngsters did fifty years earlier, our kids loved to hike "out back," often climbing to the top of Jelm Mountain where they could look out over the entire Laramie valley.

When weather and river-flow were appropriate, fishermen flocked out from town and up from Colorado. Several sportsmen decided to fish from our little beach, and the boys discovered them there. The kids couldn't allow this. They had appropriated this section of the river as our very own. They decided to scare away the fish by throwing rocks into the water, so the men would have to move on. Fred, eager to help but less capable of aim and range, threw a rock that hit one of the fishermen, denting his hat. If the men had been annoyed by the splashing rocks, they were now enraged, and took off after the kids. The boys ran for their lives, and well familiar with the woods, managed to escape. I didn't hear about it until years later.

THERE WAS A JOB TO DO,
SO I DID IT

I N MY HOMETOWN, the seasons had formed a backdrop as we
walked across the stage of life. But here at the cabin, the set
came alive around us and gathered us in. Each season had its
own scent, its own sound and colors, its own texture. The
river sang with the seasons, burbled beneath the crust of winter,
roared with springtime, lazed in the mottled sun and shadows
of summer, caught and over-spilled the leafy coins of autumn.

Most people hated the cottonwood fuzz that turned up
at the end of June or in early July. The trees turned white
with the cotton, hiding the leaves. The fuzz drifted everywhere, coated the blossoming wild roses, covered the seats of
the cars if windows were left open. On the ground, a thin
layer of fluffy white formed into drifts and rills where pushed
by the breezes.

People tracked it into their houses.

But I didn't mind the fuzz. I wondered if people really
looked at it. Unlike snow, the white was two-toned, a bright

white center surrounded by a softer white puff made of phenomenally fine, wool-like hairs. Each seed had its own fuzzy-white parachute, but together they floated like balls of cotton. One calm night it filled the air, floating in all directions. Under the almost-full moon, the cotton drifted down in the moonlight like huge, three-dimensional snowflakes, translucent and glowing. Beauty didn't annoy me, even when it made extra work.

When Ellie and Bill bought a ranch between Laramie and Cheyenne, they moved, along with the horses, the German shepherds, and Ellie's horsemanship school operations, leaving empty the big house, the barn, and other ranch facilities. Of course, we hoped to move in. This was delayed, however, because the landlord wanted to make some repairs in the kitchen and bathroom before taking on a new tenant. But we could begin using the outer buildings and corrals right away. How does that "law" go? If space is available, something will fill it?

With use of the big barn in addition to the sheds at home, our involvement with animals and 4-H mushroomed. Before I realized what was happening, we had a small flock of Rambouillet sheep and we'd also acquired more bum lambs. Our original orphan lambs were growing, even little Dinky.

With county fair coming up in early August, 4-H meetings and projects, demonstrations, and record books got into full swing. Sam continued with leathercraft and ropecraft; Frank with his insects. One year his bug box was selected to go to State Fair where it won a blue ribbon and notice from the State Agricultural Extension Entomologist: hearty congratulations tempered with the admonition, "You have one *Diptera* in your *Hymenoptera*."

When Jenny started 4-H, she was fortunate to learn sewing from an expert, a home economics instructor, wife of the college professor I'd worked with on his horse book. After the couple retired and moved to Loveland, Colorado, to raise Arabians on their farm, they invited Jenny to stay with them for a week. Roy was appalled.

"What, Jenny be away from home for a whole *week*?"

"They have three new foals," I said. "Jenny would love being there."

"Well, I don't know. What if she's unhappy? What if they're not careful around the horses? What if she misses us and gets homesick?"

"She probably won't," I said. "After all, she's ten now. Your little girl is growing up."

When we asked her if she'd like to stay with the Gormans for a week, she was all excitement. "Oh yes! It will be wonderful to get away from those stupid brothers!"

Sure enough, she spent most of her time with the horses, brushing the foals and riding one of the mares. A letter reported on other joys, as well:

I'm learning to knit. This card is made from dried flowers from the garden between waxed paper and kleenx. I helped

237

fix the electric fence Friday. It sure is nice down here in Love-land. Love, Jenny.

She didn't want to come home.

That summer, the kids showed their lambs at the fair, our first experience of showing livestock. Then Frank, with Connie's help, got into bees. Connie gave him some equipment, showed him how to set up the hive and use a smoker, and we ordered a box of honeybees. Later, we borrowed an extractor and learned how to separate honey from the combs, a project that involved making us all—and the kitchen, floor to ceiling—woefully sticky.

But as our months, then years, in the cabin stretched out, uncertainty eroded Roy's innate optimism. Sometimes his notes gave me a warm, rich feeling, a comfortable sense of love no matter what else was going on. Sometimes they tore at my heart:

Dear Gazelle. Please decide if you would like for me to go and have a chat with Roberts [concerning buying land] or stay home and work on wood today (better work on this little project alone though—dawg is sometimes influenced by hedonistic desires, or even outright poor judgment). Love, Roy. P. S. Where can we do the most good?

His thinking had shifted a little. He'd come to see that his way of living—doing things the "old way"—affected more than just himself, that "doing the most good," contributing meaningfully to family and community, might mean making some concessions. But flexibility wasn't one of his virtues. He could never see how much his logic was colored by his wishes. He never came to grips with the fact that as times changed, life-changes were required in response. His grandfather had made a good living on the farm, had raised nine kids and prospered enough to help them all get started in life. Therefore it was right for Roy, for us, to do the same. Why wasn't it working?

Although we were making some progress, he suffered from being unable to better provide for his family in the way he thought should have been possible. But he kept trying.

While I don't recall talking about it, I think Roy and I both knew instinctively that, as far as the kids were concerned, our original intentions in taking on cabin living had been fulfilled. Somehow while we grownups were fumbling through our days, the kids had developed the responsibility and ability to cope that we had originally envisioned. Proof of this caught us by surprise one day, blowing in on a wild spring storm when we drove over the Summit to Cheyenne.

The morning was fine enough, all the kids were in school, and we planned to be home before they were. I'm not sure we'd even told them we were going.

The Summit marked the highest point between Laramie and Cheyenne, a segment of U.S. 30, the original transcontinental Lincoln Highway. Sculptor Robert Russin's huge bust of Old Abe topped the crest, and the nearby Summit Tavern (before it burned down) afforded incredible views of the Pole Mountain area in the Laramie Range. The sculpture sits atop a stone base, the whole monument tall as a four-story building. It had to be dismantled and moved down from its original site when the road was rerouted as Interstate 80, then reconstructed. Even though cutting down on the steepest grades by several hundred feet, the new road was often closed by the notorious fierce weather. Plows, even if they could see where they were going, couldn't begin to keep up with the drifts.

Roy and I completed our business in the state's capital and headed back home, west on I-80.

"Oh boy," I said. "That sure doesn't look good." A bank of ominous clouds boiled up out of nowhere, the wind picked up, and fine pellets began hitting the windshield. We hurried on as snow swirled and thickened and visibility diminished. Drifts began building across the road. The 1953 pickup we drove had no four-wheel drive and no radio, or we might have heard the warnings. Only later we found out the road had been closed behind us not long after we'd started for home. But then, maybe it was just as well we didn't know. We still held hope of a plow going through to clear the way a bit.

We kept going. What else could we do? The kids would soon be getting home to a rapidly cooling house, and there were no cell phones back then to call them or anybody else. Besides, Roy enjoyed this kind of challenge and had supreme confidence that he could drive through anything. Turning back didn't occur to either of us. Hadn't we taken this kind of trip *deliberately* when we were courting all those years ago? For *fun*? Somehow, it wasn't quite the same. I wasn't *that* sure he could drive through anything.

Time dissolved into gray nothingness while we chugged along, sometimes freely except for the drag of going uphill into the wind, sometimes caught in drifts. Roy would have to back up, hit a drift again, then rock back and forth until the old truck broke through. Or he'd get out for some quick shoveling, then hit it again. I hoped nothing was coming along at full tilt behind us—this *was* an Interstate highway, after all.

I was glad the pickup's windshield wipers worked. On our old, retired Model A, the wipers (attached above the windshield) could be moved manually with a knob on the inside when the little wiper motor wasn't strong enough to do the job. But manual operation was slow, and in a bad storm, Roy often drove with his long arm out the wide-open window, clearing snow from the windshield with his hand. I shivered at the thought, glad the automatic wipers continued to work. Also, the pickup heater worked a little. Sort of.

After a while it occurred to us that traffic was light. In fact, it was nonexistent. Or maybe we just couldn't see it. We couldn't really see anything. All points of reference had disappeared. We assumed we were making progress, but it was hard to tell because we had to back up so much. Time passed.

"Can you see anything?" I asked. I thought he was driving by instinct, and hoped we were still on the road.

Sometimes he rolled down the window and stuck his head out. "Lyndon! Every now and then I can see the white line. There! It blew clear for a minute." He kept muttering "Nixon!" or the like under his breath.

After what seemed like a day or two, he said, "Ah, I think we've passed the Summit!"

I couldn't see two inches in front of the windshield. "You do? How can you tell?"

He stuck his head out the window again, and when he pulled it back, he said, "We've got to be going downhill. The engine's having an easier time of it."

Lost in the whiteout of nothingness, I thought back through the years to our return trip from Vermont with four little kids in the two vintage vehicles. Then we'd parked somewhere around this very spot and gazed out over endless miles of plains, hills, and mountains. We'd noted the Big Laramie River winding through the floor of the valley below. Roy had pointed out Jelm Mountain and said he hoped we'd find a home at the foot of it. I'd vaguely remembered having seen the huge log ranchhouses there along the river just beyond Harmony but never suspected how, in the intervening near-decade, our lives would come to fill that vision. What I wouldn't have given for a fraction of that clarity now in this storm.

Our surroundings had been darkening for hours, and when we finally drove through Laramie, night had fallen and swirls of light haloed each streetlamp. Only twenty-five miles to go. So far we'd spent at least five hours on the road to cover about fifty miles. I tried not to imagine what might be happening at home.

When, several hours later, we staggered in the door, the dog greeted us rapturously. But then, she'd have done that even if we'd only been gone two minutes. The kids hardly noticed. They had fires burning in both stoves, and the house was cozy and warm. The woodbox was full. They'd made supper, cleaned up and piled the dishes neatly in the sink, taken care of livestock chores, fed the dog and cats, and now sat reading or doing homework. They weren't even curious about where we'd been. A bit piqued, I wondered if they'd notice if we were gone a week. But I was proud of them.

I thought of a story Connie Hansen told. He'd been twelve years old when his family lived on a remote little ranch in the mountains. After a tough winter, their supplies were about gone. When the weather broke, Connie's parents took the horse and wagon for the long trip to town, with enough errands to keep them both busy, leaving him alone. They'd be back by the next morning. Another storm blew in and they couldn't get home for ten days. Connie shoveled, chopped wood, kept the fire going, took care of the livestock, and fed himself with the only food left in the house — potatoes. He fried them, boiled them, baked them, invented new ways to cook them. He took care of the ranch as was expected, both by his parents and by himself. But he couldn't stand the sight of potatoes for a long time afterward.

This was the kind of self-sufficiency and ability to cope that I admired so much in our neighbors, old and young, and what Roy and I wanted for our kids. Well, they had sure coped this time. It felt good to know they could handle something unexpected that tested their capabilities without overwhelming them. But mostly, the learning experience was mine. Okay, Ma, you don't *have* to be here all the time! They were maturing, learning the basic living skills they'd need later on. Step back and let it happen.

And happen it did. From this time at the cabin by the Big Laramie river, they gained a sense that no matter what situation presented itself, "a way" was possible, that even if all current systems broke down (loss of power, social structure, whatever), they could meet the challenge.

In November 1970 we finally moved into the big house. Fourteen big rooms with high ceilings and carved woodwork; a bathroom with hot and cold running water; a roomy kitchen; dining room; living room with its bank of windows opening to the south and the river; a library; a bedroom downstairs (for Roy and me); and another room for crafts and projects. A circular staircase led up to a large hallway and four bedrooms for kids and another for a guestroom. I exulted in the joy of spreading out, with each of us having our own space, of finally being able to unpack boxes that had been piled up since Vermont (except for Hopelessly Miscellaneous. I think that's still sitting around somewhere).

Even so, I had to stretch my imagination to envision what it must have been like so many years earlier when Wes Johnson wrote about the first residents of the big house, the Sodergreens, in his memoirs. "To supplement income, Mrs. Sodergreen kept paying guests through the summer months. The fishing on the Big Laramie was very good and she had many folks from as far away as Denver. Most of these people came by horse and buggy from Laramie, as the auto was just coming into use. After the autos got more popular and folks could go farther afield, the end of the summer resort business resolved into Sunday dinners for as many as seventy-five people. And when I talk about dinners, they were really out of this world! These folks had large gardens so that there were a lot of fresh vegetables. Fish was the main dish. There was also lots of homegrown chicken, beef, and pork, home-made ice cream and pies of all kinds. All of this feast for seventy-five cents. No wonder the bankers, lawyers, merchants, doctors and many others came out for Sunday dinner. I believe some of these people starved for two days so they could eat more."

The following spring, we witnessed another seasonal phenomenon: the return of the bats. For months they swooped and flitted at dusk, stirring the air and startling the humans. If it hadn't been for the bats, I think our mosquitoes would have been even thicker than they were. I wondered how many pounds or millions of the ferocious insects were consumed by the bats.

245

The little beasts lived in the attic of the big house. Years earlier, concerned about rabies and the safety of her summer school students, Ellie had contacted some bat experts from the university. In a multi-year study, the scientists discovered that the colony migrated from caves in New Mexico. These were females only, and they came north to birth and raise their young, then all returned in the fall to their home caves in the south. They were clean, healthy, and disease-free.

As the youngsters grew, they began flying with their mamas. Each year at least one of the bat-kids couldn't find her way back into their attic nursery and ended up swooping around the living room or kitchen. This, of course, sent the students scrambling and screaming in delicious terror.

The tradition continued after we moved into the big house, and one year we almost ended up with a bat pet. Perhaps she was a slow-learner, or else she relished the excitement. At any rate, she made a habit of zooming into the kitchen at supper time and swooping around and around over our heads. At first this made for a lot of harrowing excitement as we shouted, ran to open the door, grabbed for brooms, and tried to haze the bat out into the entryway, then close the door behind her. From there we could open the outside door to let her out. Toots loved it. She wheeled around the kitchen as well, bouncing off the cabinets and leaping wildly with one paw and all claws extended, trying to catch the flying mouse (never did). Peggy, perhaps annoyed that she couldn't join the aerial dance, contributed by barking.

After several days of this, things settled into a fairly pleasant routine. The little bat flew in, zoomed around the room (encouraged by Toots), and apparently waited for us to open the doors, at which point she left. On a few occasions, this drama added an agreeable (for us) spice to our company dinners.

"Eeek! What's that!?"

"Oh, that's just our trained bat," one of the kids would say. We calmly continued eating while the company leaped up and started shouting, "What'll we do! Where's a broom? Can you hit it?" Toots contributed her cat ballet to the commotion, Peggy barked, the company scrambled, the kids laughed, and Roy or I would open the doors.

"Come on, sweetie. Time to go." Responding beautifully, she sailed out into the night. Apparently mama watched for her outside and called to her because only once did our little bat make a second run at the kitchen.

Toots kept having kittens, but now the old cat appreciated compassion. If the dog wasn't on hand, I'd have to hold her paw. When she had her final litter, Peggy stood by to help lick the kittens dry. Toots felt so benign, she even licked Peggy's nose. She and Herbert raised the kittens with Peggy's help, but several months later, both old cats passed away, a few weeks of each other. We buried Herbert at home with due ceremony.

I carried Toots, wrapped in a baby blanket, to the Hansen place. West of the river, rocky hills rose sharp and steep to the Medicine Bow National Forest boundary. The land was cut by deep ravines that spilled creeks into the river and blazed orange and yellow with aspens in the fall. Ridges rose between them, and Connie called the tallest of these Wildcat Mountain.

It took me a while, skirting the pines and scrambling among the rocks and sagebrush, to reach the top of Wildcat Mountain. The wind whipped my clothes, shrieked through the pines below, and sent cloud-shadows riding the river and scudding across the landscape. To the east lay Jelm Mountain and the distant haze of Colorado. I found a place where a pile of loose rock, perhaps the remains of a shepherd's cairn, raised a natural monument. Moving aside a few stones to form a cavity, I laid the slight body in gently and replaced the stones. Time then to take a few moments to offer up a prayer for my friend and to bless the fury of the wind, the name of the mountain, and the wildness of the setting. Toots would have loved it all.

※ ⌒ ※ ⌒ ※ ⌒ ※

None of us really felt a sense of loss in leaving the cabin. The kids celebrated having their own rooms at last, and we all rejoiced in real plumbing. The big kitchen had a usable wood stove (we could all keep our wood-cutting skills honed), but also an electric range and oven. We hadn't so much moved *away*—the cabin was still there in sight and the kids still had their favorite haunts—as shifted over to a more solid lifestyle. An apple tree grew by the door, and out back at the edge of the lawn, the Big Laramie murmured and slapped against the rocks. I grew to love the big house more and more (bats and all) over the seven years we lived there while the kids progressed through Harmony school and then through high school in town.

The river was even closer here than before. I could cross the lawn, stand at the river's edge and look upstream to the bridge, or glance back over my shoulder at the house. Closer, always comforting and encouraging, but less intimate.

I thought of the cabin with affection, kind of the way I thought back on my childhood: an experience cherished but outgrown, one to remember sometimes with pain but more often with warmth and laughter. Now and then Peggy and I walked back past the cabin and followed the path to our little beach. While the dog splashed and played in the water, I settled back on the grass and listened to the robins, the flickers and killdeers, blackbirds and magpies, and watched the cliff swallows as they swooped overhead.

I held my hand out to let the cottonwood fuzz settle on my palm and then waft away. I'd bring an old coat to sit on when frost iced the grass and willows with lace. The brilliance of the stained-glass leaves of autumn took my breath away as they preened against the deep-bright sky and then, liberated by a gust of wind, broke free to fill the air. I watched them settle on the stream to begin their life journey downriver.

With my heart full to bursting, I listened to the river sing.

When asked many years later what the cabin experience meant to them, the kids focused on a sense of competence, a confidence in their own ability to cope. Fred mentioned an incident that happened when he was sixteen. We were in the process of moving to our own finally acquired ranch in the north part of the state. Sam and Jenny had already left "the nest" and were on their own. Fred was alone on the new place (in order to start school on time; he still had two years of high school left), while Frank kept track of livestock at the old place, and Roy and I shuttled back and forth with truck and stock trailer, moving our animals and belongings. Roy had ordered a semi-load of hay to be delivered, preparing for the livestock's arrival, and assured the driver he'd be there to help unload. With typical slowness, Roy didn't leave Laramie on time, so Fred was left to help the driver unload and stack the 700 or more sixty- to seventy-pound bales. As they finished, the amazed driver announced, "I've never seen a sixteen-year-old kid who could keep up with me before."

Fred was surprised there was even cause for comment. "There was a job to do, so I did it."

The kids also said they reaped another benefit from those years. They felt that through the cabin experience, they had become hooked on nature and the outdoors—all the glories of God's creation. And they could pass that love of beauty along to their own children.

In later years, Fred wrote:

The land etched itself into my soul. When I think of Laramie, I think much more of the land than the people, because the land dominated the people. In my mind, I mostly see

Laramie as a thin dark line far across the prairie, in the shadow of the Laramie Range, from a rocky outcrop on Jelm Mountain—my backyard playground from the age of about ten to sixteen. I think of the antelope flashing their white butts and dashing away. Mule deer bucks fighting over a doe. The wind howling across the plains and covering them in a moving blanket of snow three feet high during ground blizzards. The incredible feast of stars on a moonless winter night. Laramie is 7500 feet high—close to 8000 twenty-five miles to the southwest where I grew up—and the stars there are incredible. The Milky Way was my companion, a white path across the sky.

The kids were ready to step into the future with their own dreams. We need those dreams, even if the reality doesn't always match up—like that horseback ride I had along the highway punctuated by the semi driver with his air horn.

Here by the Laramie River, blessed by its solace and nourishment, Roy and I had both learned at least as much as the kids. The cabin years taught us a lot about hardness and beauty, challenge and patience, frustration and fulfillment.

We both learned to hang on. We knew the kids would, too.

ACKNOWLEDGMENTS

Over the many years this book has been in the making, family members and friends have read chapters or whole drafts. They have shared their ideas, memories, insights, editorial expertise, and suggestions, all of which have woven a thread or pleat into the final fabric of story.

My profound thanks for their interest, input, and encouragement go to Ellin K. Roberts, Jeanne Williams, Peggy Robinson, Linda and Doug Nelson, Sam Collier, Seda Collier, Jenny Gilbertson, Katy Collier, Eleanor Prince, and Mark Young. Special thanks also to Margaret and Everett Johnson for sharing and allowing me to quote from family memoirs. For professional editorial work, I'm indebted and deeply grateful to Linda M. Hasselstrom and Andi Hummel, Judy Plazyk, and Laura McCormick.

Warmest thanks to the Bearlodge Writers who have shepherded this work through chapter upon rewritten chapter with patience, good humor, and an eye to improving every page, sentence, and word. Many thanks, also, to the staff at Crook County Public Library who always came through with answers. My gratitude to Nancy Curtis of High Plains Press knows no bounds, for electing to publish this work and for her precision, care, judgment, and skill in its editing and production.

What a joy and blessing it has been for me to work with all of you!

FURTHER READING

The following books were helpful to my writing and provide additional information on the Harmony area.

Albany County Cow-Belles. *Cow-Belles Ring School Bells: A History of Rural Schools in Albany County, Wyoming.* Nov. 1976.

Conrad Hansen. *I Remember: Stories of Wyoming.* Jelm Mountain Publications, 1976.

Johnson, Geil. Unpublished manuscript, no date.

Johnson, Wesley. *Early Days on the Laramie.* Unpublished manuscript, 1973.

The Midwest Review, Vol. 7, No. 3, March 1926. Published for Midwest Family by the Midwest Refining Company, Casper, Wyoming.

Moore, Vandi. *Brands on the Boswell.* High Plains Press, 1986.

Olson, Ted. *Ranch on the Laramie: A Memoir of an American Boyhood.* Atlantic-Little, Brown, 1973.

Gaydell Collier lives on her ranch in Wyoming's Black Hills where the family moved after leaving the Harmony community in 1977. Inspired by the beauty of land and wildlife, she writes, walks the hills with her dog Maxie, and looks forward to visits from children, grandchildren, and great-grandchildren.

Gaydell co-authored three books on horses and horsemanship for Doubleday (including *Basic Horsemanship: English and Western*) and co-edited three collections of women's writing for Houghton-Mifflin (including *Leaning Into the Wind*). Her essays, articles, and poetry have appeared in a variety of publications and anthologies, and she has given numerous workshops and presentations on journaling, memoir, and women's writing in the West. In 2004 she received the Wyoming Governor's Arts Award for Literature.

~ NOTES ON THE PRODUCTION OF THE BOOK ~

This book was simultaneously released in two editions.

A *limited edition* of only 200 copies was Smyth sewn
with headbands of blue and cream,
bound in Flutterby Blue Kivar 7 in the Skiver pattern,
embossed with Sundance gold foil,
and wrapped in a full-color dustjacket.
Each copy is hand-numbered and signed by the author.

The *softcover trade edition* is covered with ten-point stock,
printed in four colors, and coated with a scuff-free matte finish.

The text of both editions is from the Adobe Garamond Family.
Display type is Adobe Trajan and Oldstyle Chewed
by the Electronic Typographer with Insecta and Poetica ornaments.

The book is printed on fifty-five-pound Nature's Natural,
an acid-free, recycled paper, by Thomson-Shore.